# NORDSTROM
# FAMILY TABLE COOKBOOK

## SHARING TASTE AND FLAVOR

Michael Northern

PHOTOGRAPHS BY NOEL BARNHURST

CHRONICLE BOOKS

SAN FRANCISCO

ISBN: 978-1-4521-0737-0

Manufactured in China.

Design and typesetting: Gretchen Scoble
Food stylist: George Dolese
Food styling assistant: Elisabet der Nederlanden
Prop stylist: Glenn Jenkins

KitchenAid is a registered trademark of KitchenAid. Maldon is a registered trademark of Maldon Crystal Salt Company Limited. Nordstrom Makers is a trademark of Nordstrom.

10 9 8 7 6 5 4 3 2 1

Published exclusively for Nordstrom, Inc., by Chronicle Books LLC.

Chronicle Books LLC
680 Second Street
San Francisco, CA 94107

www.chroniclebooks.com/custom

# Dedication

To Jarod Michael Northern, whose warm, wonderful smile
simply lights up our family table.

# Contents

## BEEF, PORK, LAMB & VEAL    85

Skirt Steak with Romesco Sauce and Balsamic Roast Onions    87

Grilled Rib-Eye Steaks with Chipotle Lime Butter    89

Steak al Forno    90

Sixth & Pine Meatloaf    93

Beef Bourguignon    95

Grilled Skirt Steak with Cilantro Lime Vinaigrette    97

Short Ribs Provençal    98

Blue Cheese Sirloin Burgers    99

Osso Buco    100

Slow-Roasted Pork with Pickled Ginger Cherry Sauce    101

Double-Cut Pork Chops with Char Siu Sauce    102

Greek-Marinated Pork Tenderloin with Tzatziki    104

Pork Chile Verde    106

Wisconsin-Style Bratwurst with Caraway Sauerkraut    108

Sausage, Tomato, and Polenta Casserole    110

Peppercorn-Crusted Lamb Chops with Spicy Fig Jam    112

## CHICKEN    115

Sixth & Pine Seasoned Fried Chicken    117

New Orleans Chicken and Andouille Étouffée    119

Herb Roasted Chicken Breasts    121

Grilled Mediterranean Chicken with Lemon-Herb Marinade    122

Chicken Breasts Sautéed in Apple Cider    125

Chicken and Mushroom Piccata    127

Bánh Mì Vietnamese Spicy Chicken Sandwiches    129

Grilled Chicken Breasts with Red Chili Marinade    131

Grilled Chicken Burgers    132

## SEAFOOD    135

Roast Salmon with Tuscan Marinade    136

Horseradish Crusted Salmon    138

Soy and Mirin Glazed Salmon    139

Halibut Steaks Roasted in Ginger Soy Broth    141

Shrimp with Honey, Lemon, and Caper Sauce    142

Grilled Tamarind Shrimp Kebabs    143

Thai Steamed Mussels    144

Crab Macaroni and Cheese    146

## PASTA & RISOTTO    149

Penne with Bolognese Sauce    150

Perfect Meatballs with Tomato-Garlic Sauce    153

Linguine with White Clam Sauce    155

Shrimp and Lobster Carbonara    156

Angel Hair Arrabiata with Crab and Lemon Oil    158

Pasta Margherita    159

Pappardelle Primavera    161

Spring Vegetable Risotto    163

Baked Rigatoni with Spinach and Fresh Mozzarella    165

Gnocchi with Italian Sausage and Tomato Alfredo Sauce    166

Homemade Fresh Egg Pasta    168

# Preface

Nordstrom Family Table Cookbook: Sharing Taste and Flavor *is our fourth cookbook and follows in the footsteps of our three earlier efforts,* Nordstrom Friends and Family, Nordstrom Entertaining at Home, *and* Nordstrom Flavors. *We are thrilled and humbled by the reception these cookbooks have received. It is proof of the special role great food can play in our lives.*

*This book is a compendium of fresh and flavorful recipes gathered from our team in the restaurant division as well as from their families. Our aim here is to provide wonderful yet down-to-earth recipes that are ideally suited for home cooking and sharing with loved ones.*

*A great recipe is only as good as its practicality and approachability. Therefore, we filled the book with recipes that are easy to shop for, without challenging multistore excursions for rare ingredients or unusual cooking equipment.*

*What makes this cookbook unique is the care and attention given to the smallest details, which guarantee that the recipes will work every time you use them. These well-written recipes are based on clear and practical methods that are easy to understand.*

*Our first cookbook was created, in part, as a response to recipe requests for favorite menu offerings that our customers wanted to re-create at home.* Nordstrom Family Table Cookbook *honors this theme and features some of our newest recipes as well as a few beloved old favorites that were not in the previous books.*

*From the very first day Nordstrom was founded over one hundred years ago as a little shoe store in downtown Seattle, it has been our aim to do our best to take care of our customers. With the opening of our first restaurant in 1973, food became a special way to share this simple philosophy. Over the years, our restaurants and menus have evolved with the times, but our goal remains the same. This book, along with our other cookbooks, exemplifies our devotion to our customers from the time of our modest food and beverage origins almost forty years ago.*

*We offer these recipes with the hope that they will become cherished family favorites, constantly requested and enjoyed at the family table for generations to come.*

—Erik Nordstrom
*President of Stores*

# Introduction

*The simple act of sharing food elevates cooking to a culinary art and makes food special. Gatherings of friends and family are the "canvas" that the home cook paints on, the "pages" that the cook writes in. Without gatherings around the family table we might find less reason to cook, and it is certainly true that very little artistry would be needed. This collection of recipes celebrates the love we feel for our families and those we welcome into our homes. Great cooking isn't about showmanship but rather about sharing unpretentious food and enjoying the fruits of our labors.*

*The Nordstrom Family Table Cookbook draws its inspiration from the importance of the family table in daily life and is a compilation of unpretentious dishes that the contributors serve in their own homes. The family table is where we gather to break bread and enjoy one another's company. In today's bustling world, making the time to enjoy meals together at the table is often sidetracked by conflicting schedules, after-school activities, and work commitments. But when we eat together, the bonds of family and friendship are strengthened.*

*Food is meant to be shared; somehow it tastes better when enjoyed with those who are close to us. And cooking is the source that nourishes a culture and keeps it strong. This cookbook offers simple, down-to-earth recipes to share at the family table with the hope that you will find new favorites to add to your repertoire.*

*Many of the recipes in the Nordstrom Family Table Cookbook were gathered from Nordstrom's talented restaurant division employees and their families. These are the dishes that they prepare for their own home meals, and many of them have become family traditions. These special recipes are presented along with those for popular Nordstrom restaurant dishes that have not been published in any of the three earlier Nordstrom cookbooks. All of them are simple to prepare and casual in nature, perfect for the home cook. These dishes are meant to be served family style, passed from one end of the table to the other and casually shared at mealtime with a minimum of fuss.*

The book is organized by chapters including Small Plates, Starters & Nibbles; Soups & Small Salads; Main-Course Salads; Beef, Pork, Lamb & Veal; Chicken; Seafood; Pasta & Risotto; Side Dishes & Breads; and Desserts. Our hope is that you will encounter recipes that capture your interest and then easily find complementary dishes or simple recipes that offer contrast, such as the rustic served alongside something more formal, a salad served with a dish prepared on the grill, or the perfect dessert to enhance a menu you have planned. Many of the dishes celebrate the seasons of the year, inviting you to follow your instincts and plan your menus with taste and flavor in mind.

The time, energy, and passion that Nordstrom lavishes on its restaurants and espresso bars is a testament to how we feel about the importance of offering food to our guests. Our restaurants and coffee bars add an important dimension to shopping at Nordstrom: they offer a comfortable oasis and a convenient meeting place for friends and family. The welcome touch of a well-prepared meal is just another version of the family table, which we humbly offer to our guests as part of the experience of shopping at Nordstrom. The goal of this book was to capture some of the tastes and flavors offered at our restaurants along with those our chefs prepare for their own friends and family, and to make them available for our customers to serve at home.

As a chef, I find that many people are intimidated to cook for me, feeling that their efforts may somehow not stand up to scrutiny. I can assure you that I and every chef I know are more than grateful to have a home-cooked meal served to us without pretension. Three of my favorite words, in fact, are "Dinner is served."

I hope you will enjoy these special dishes and find both comfort and joy in preparing them for those you love, and that many of these recipes will become your family favorites.

—Michael Northern

# SMALL PLATES, STARTERS & NIBBLES

# Rosemary Grilled Artichokes with Lemon Dipping Sauce

*↜ contributed by* PETER O'KEEFE

*My grandmother had lemon trees and rosemary in her garden that flourished in Laguna Beach's Mediterranean-like weather. With this memory in mind, every spring, when citrus season is winding down, my family gorges on a feast of first-crop artichokes, joined by lemons and rosemary. In my version, they are finished on the grill for a smoky note.* {MAKES 4 SERVINGS}

2 lemons

2 cups mayonnaise

1 tablespoon finely chopped fresh
   flat-leaf parsley

2 teaspoons Dijon mustard

4 globe artichokes, preferably with
   stems attached

⅓ cup extra-virgin olive oil

8 cloves garlic, very finely minced

2 tablespoons finely chopped fresh
   rosemary

Flaky sea salt, such as fleur de sel de
   Guérande or Maldon salt, for finishing

Lemon wedges for serving

1. Grate the zest from the lemons and reserve. Juice the lemons; you should have about ½ cup lemon juice.

2. To make a dipping sauce, mix the mayonnaise, the lemon zest, ¼ cup of the lemon juice, the parsley, and mustard together in a small bowl. Cover and refrigerate for at least 1 hour or up to 3 days.

3. Bring a large pot of salted water to a boil over high heat. Meanwhile, prepare the artichokes: Mix the remaining ¼ cup lemon juice with 6 cups of cold water in a deep bowl. For each artichoke, pare off the dark green skin with a paring knife if the stem is attached and use kitchen scissors to snip off the spiky tips of the outer leaves. Cut the artichoke in half lengthwise. Immediately submerge the artichoke halves in the lemon water. Repeat with the remaining artichokes.

4. Drain the artichokes and add to the boiling water. Cover and return to a boil. Reduce the heat to medium and uncover. Cook at a brisk simmer until a bottom leaf can be easily pulled from an artichoke, about 18 minutes. Do not overcook the artichokes, or they will fall apart during grilling. Drain the artichokes and rinse under cold running water. Drain again, and transfer to a large bowl of ice water to cool completely. Drain a final time.

5. Gently squeeze each artichoke half to remove excess water. Pat dry with paper towels. Using a teaspoon, scoop out the choke and discard. Mix the olive oil, garlic, and rosemary together in a small bowl. Spoon about 2 teaspoons of the olive oil mixture over the cut sides of the artichokes and rub it into the leaves and hearts. Let stand while preparing the grill.

*continued >*

6. Prepare a medium fire in a charcoal grill, or preheat a gas grill to medium (see Note). Brush the grill grate clean. Place the artichoke halves, cut side down, on the grate. You may have some flare-ups from the dripping oil, but this is normal. Close the grill lid and cook until the artichokes are heated through and seared with grill marks, about 5 minutes. Flip the artichokes and sear the other side, 2 to 3 minutes.

7. Transfer the dipping sauce to 4 individual serving bowls. For each serving, place 2 artichoke halves on a plate and sprinkle with the sea salt. Serve warm with the lemon wedges and lemon dipping sauce, providing a large communal bowl for the spent leaves.

# Chicken Pot Stickers with Sweet Soy Dipping Sauce

🍴 *contributed by* JASON LONGFIELD

*While you can buy pot stickers, nothing beats the flavor and succulence of homemade fried dumplings. Pot stickers are fun to make, especially if you get youngsters involved to help fold the wrappers and filling together into plump pillows.* {MAKES 6 SERVINGS}

### SWEET SOY DIPPING SAUCE

¾ cup soy sauce

¼ cup packed light brown sugar

2 tablespoons granulated sugar

2 tablespoons bottled ponzu sauce (available at Asian markets)

2 tablespoons seasoned rice wine vinegar

2 teaspoons Chinese chili garlic paste or sambal oelek

2 teaspoons Asian sesame oil

### CHICKEN FILLING

1 pound boneless, skinless chicken thighs, cut into 1-inch chunks, or 1 pound ground chicken (not ground chicken breast)

1 tablespoon plus 1½ teaspoons soy sauce

1 large egg white, lightly beaten

1 tablespoon minced green onion, white part only (reserve green parts for garnish)

2 teaspoons peeled and minced fresh ginger

1. To make the Sweet Soy Dipping Sauce, whisk all of the ingredients together in a medium bowl. Cover and refrigerate for at least 2 hours to blend the flavors. (The sauce can be refrigerated for up to 5 days.)

2. To make the Chicken Filling, put the chicken on a baking sheet and freeze until firm but not frozen, about 1 hour. In batches, pulse in a food processor fitted with the metal blade until coarsely ground. Transfer to a medium bowl. Add the remaining ingredients and mix well.

3. Line a large baking sheet with parchment or waxed paper and dust well with cornstarch. Place a wonton wrapper on the work surface in front of you. Lightly brush the edges of the wrapper with the beaten egg. Place a heaping teaspoon of filling in the center of the wrapper. Fold the wrapper over to meet the opposite edge, then pleat and pinch the edges closed. Stand the pot sticker, pleated edges up, on the prepared baking sheet. Repeat with the remaining filling and wrappers. (The pot stickers can be loosely covered with plastic wrap and refrigerated for up to 3 hours.)

4. Heat the oil in a very large nonstick skillet over medium-high heat. Place the pot stickers, pleated edges up, in the skillet. Add ½ cup water and cover tightly. Cook until the water has evaporated and the pot stickers are sizzling, about 8 minutes. Uncover and cook until the pot stickers are nicely browned on the bottom, about 2 minutes longer.

*continued >*

1½ teaspoons Chinese chili garlic paste or sambal oelek

2 cloves garlic, minced

½ teaspoon kosher salt


Cornstarch for dusting

36 round wonton (gyoza) wrappers

1 large egg, beaten

3 tablespoons canola oil

1 green onion, green parts only, thinly sliced on the diagonal (reserved from filling)

2 tablespoons sesame seeds, toasted (see page 27)

5. Pour the sauce into 6 ramekins or custard cups for dipping the pot stickers. Divide the pot stickers among 6 soup bowls. Sprinkle with the sliced green onion leaves and the sesame seeds. Serve hot, with a ramekin of dipping sauce for each person.

# Ceviche with Seaweed and Chipotle

*contributed by* REY EMILIO GARCIA LEMUS

*Although ceviche is served throughout Latin America, it reaches its apogee in Peru, where it is made with all manner of sparkling-fresh seafood. I learned to make it early in my professional food career, and I still love it, especially as a cold and refreshing first course on a hot summer day. My version combines traditional Latin flavors with Asian accents.* {MAKES 6 SERVINGS}

1 cup fresh lime juice, plus 2 tablespoons

1 teaspoon kosher salt, plus more to taste

1 pound rockfish or red snapper fillets, cut into ½-inch cubes

1 tablespoon black peppercorns

1 bay leaf

1 pound large (21/25 count) shrimp, peeled and deveined

¼ cup ¼-inch-diced red bell pepper

¼ cup ¼-inch-diced yellow bell pepper

¼ cup seeded and ¼-inch-diced plum (Roma) tomato

3 tablespoons finely chopped fresh cilantro

1 teaspoon finely chopped fresh mint

1 tablespoon adobo sauce from canned chipotle chiles in adobo

Freshly ground black pepper

2 cups Japanese-style seaweed salad, available at natural foods stores and Asian markets

1 lime, cut into sixths, for garnish

1. Mix the 1 cup lime juice and the salt together in a nonreactive medium bowl. Add the fish and stir to combine. Cover with plastic wrap and refrigerate, stirring occasionally, until opaque, at least 4 or up to 6 hours.

2. Meanwhile, bring 3 quarts water and the peppercorns and bay leaf to a boil in a large saucepan over high heat. Add the shrimp and cook until firm and opaque, about 3 minutes. Drain and rinse under cold running water. Transfer to a small bowl and cover with plastic wrap. Refrigerate until chilled, at least 2 hours.

3. Drain the fish, discarding the marinade, and return to the bowl. Add the shrimp, red and yellow bell peppers, tomato, cilantro, and mint. Mix the remaining 2 tablespoons lime juice and the chipotle adobo sauce together in a small bowl and add to the fish mixture. Stir well and season with the pepper and more salt, if needed.

4. Divide the seaweed salad among 6 chilled martini glasses or individual glass serving bowls. Top with equal amounts of the ceviche. Garnish each with a lime wedge and serve chilled.

# Spicy Black Pepper Wings

*contributed by* PETER O'KEEFE

*I learned this recipe from a Vietnamese chef, and love the combination of crispy wings and spicy sauce. If you are afraid this might be too spicy, you should know that I serve it to my toddler daughter, who appreciates it more with every tasting. To make this a meal, serve blanched green beans and steamed rice alongside.* {MAKES 4 SERVINGS}

**BLACK PEPPER SAUCE**

3 tablespoons black peppercorns

1 tablespoon canola or vegetable oil

¼ cup minced shallots

¼ cup peeled and minced fresh ginger

6 cloves garlic, minced

2 tablespoons red wine vinegar

½ cup soy sauce

Canola oil for deep-frying

16 chicken wings, chopped apart at the
   joints, wing tips discarded

¼ cup canned coconut milk, well shaken

Kosher salt

1 small red jalapeño chile, cut into
   thin rings

1. To make the Black Pepper Sauce, heat a medium skillet over medium heat. Add the peppercorns and cook, stirring occasionally, until you see a wisp of smoke and they smell very fragrant, about 1 minute. Transfer to a plate and let cool. Grind the peppercorns in an electric spice grinder or with a mortar and pestle to the consistency of fine sand.

2. Heat the canola oil in a medium skillet over medium-low heat. Add the shallots, ginger, and garlic. Cover and cook, stirring often, until tender, about 10 minutes. Increase the heat to high. Add the vinegar and cook, uncovered, until the vinegar evaporates, about 1 minute. Add the soy sauce and boil until reduced by half, about 3 minutes. Stir in the pepper and cook until slightly thickened, about 1 minute. Remove from the heat.

3. Position a rack in the center of the oven and preheat the oven to 200°F. Line a baking sheet with a brown paper bag.

4. Pour enough canola oil in a large, deep saucepan to come 3 inches up the sides and heat to 350°F on a deep-frying thermometer. In batches without crowding, add the chicken wings and cook until golden brown and cooked through, about 3½ minutes. Using a wire-mesh skimmer or slotted spoon, transfer the wings to the prepared pan. Keep warm in the oven while frying the remaining wings.

5. Just before serving, whisk the coconut milk into the black pepper mixture and reheat over medium heat. If the sauce is too thick, gradually stir in water, 1 teaspoon at a time, as needed. Transfer the wings to a large bowl. Add the sauce and toss to coat. Sprinkle a light dusting of salt over the wings.

6. For each serving, place 8 wing pieces on a plate and garnish with jalapeño rings.

# Tempura Shrimp with Dark Cherry Sauce

*✂ contributed by* RICHARD SILVA

*Shatteringly crisp tempura shrimp (the secret is ice-cold batter) is a guaranteed crowd-pleaser, and this is a popular appetizer at our flagship Bistro N restaurant in Dallas. Instead of the familiar soy dip, we offer a sweet-and-sour cherry glaze with an unexpected kick from Asian chili sauce. With zesty Sriracha sauce as a garnish, the amount of heat to apply is up to you!* {MAKES 6 SERVINGS}

DARK CHERRY SAUCE

1 teaspoon canola oil

2 cloves garlic, minced

½ cup seasoned rice wine vinegar

1 cup cherry preserves

1 teaspoon Chinese chili garlic paste


TEMPURA BATTER

1 large egg yolk

1 cup ice water

1 cup all-purpose flour

1½ teaspoons cornstarch

½ teaspoon baking powder

½ teaspoon kosher salt

1 teaspoon canola oil


Canola oil for deep-frying

36 extra-large (16/20 count) shrimp (about 2 pounds), peeled and deveined, tail segments intact

Sriracha chili sauce for garnish

1. To make the Dark Cherry Sauce, in a heavy medium saucepan, heat the canola oil over medium heat. Add the garlic and cook, stirring constantly, until golden, about 1 minute. Add the vinegar, bring to a boil, and cook until the vinegar is foamy and has reduced to about 2 tablespoons, about 10 minutes. Stir in the preserves and bring to a boil. Cook, stirring often, until lightly thickened, about 3 minutes. Stir in ¼ cup water and the chili paste. Transfer to a bowl and let cool.

2. To make the Tempura Batter, in a medium bowl whisk together the egg yolk and ice water. Sift the flour, cornstarch, baking powder, and salt together. Gradually stir in the flour mixture to make a loose, clinging batter. Stir in the canola oil. Nestle the bowl in a larger bowl of ice water and place near the stove.

3. Preheat the oven to 200°F. Line a rimmed baking sheet with paper towels. Pour enough oil into a large, deep saucepan to come 3 inches up the sides and heat to 350°F on a deep-frying thermometer.

4. In batches without crowding, add the shrimp to the batter. One at a time, remove each shrimp by its tail from the batter, letting the excess batter drip into the bowl, and quickly and carefully add to the hot oil. Deep-fry until golden brown, about 2½ minutes. Use a wire-mesh skimmer or slotted spoon to transfer the shrimp to the prepared baking sheet and keep warm in the oven while frying the remaining shrimp.

5. Pour the sauce into 6 small ramekins. Divide the shrimp among 6 serving plates and add a ramekin. Squirt several small pools of the Sriracha onto each plate as a garnish. Serve immediately with the sauce for dipping, inviting guests to use the hot sauce on the plate to increase the spiciness as they wish.

# Ahi Tuna Poke

*contributed by* JEFF BARKWILL

*Latin cuisine has ceviche, and Hawaiian cooking has poke (POH-keh), a refreshing appetizer of chilled raw fish. The difference? Poke does not include an acid ingredient to "cook" the fish. This dish is great when served with deep-fried wonton chips seasoned with salt and pepper to provide crunch, although rice or sesame crackers are good, too.* {MAKES 6 TO 8 SERVINGS}

**2 pounds ahi-grade tuna fillet**

**¾ cup reduced-sodium soy sauce**

**1 tablespoon Asian sesame oil**

**3 green onions, including green parts, thinly sliced on the diagonal**

**½ cup finely chopped sweet onion, preferably Maui**

**1 tablespoon peeled and finely shredded fresh ginger (use the small holes on a box shredder)**

**1 small chile, such as serrano, seeded and minced**

**1 tablespoon sesame seeds, toasted (see Notes)**

**Fried wontons (see Notes) or rice or sesame crackers for serving**

1. Cut the tuna into ¾-inch cubes. Cover and refrigerate.

2. Whisk the soy sauce and sesame oil together in a nonreactive medium bowl. Add the green onions, onion, ginger, and chile. Add the tuna and toss well. Cover and refrigerate for 1 hour.

3. Divide the poke among dinner plates. Sprinkle with the sesame seeds. Serve chilled, with the fried wontons.

**NOTES:** To toast sesame seeds, in a small dry skillet over medium heat, cook the sesame seeds, stirring occasionally, until toasted, about 3 minutes. Transfer to a plate and let cool.

To deep-fry wontons, pour enough vegetable oil into a large, deep saucepan to come 3 inches up the sides, and heat to 350°F on a deep-frying thermometer. Cut the wonton squares crosswise into triangles. A few at a time, add the wonton triangles to the oil and deep-fry until golden, 15 to 30 seconds. Using a wire-mesh skimmer or slotted spoon, transfer the wontons to paper towels to drain. Sprinkle with salt and pepper to taste.

# Savory Cheese Puffs with Parmesan and Ham

*~ contributed by* MICHAEL LYLE

*My nana used to bake these cheese puffs, perfect as a before-dinner nibble with a glass of wine. I could never pronounce their French name,* gougères *(goo-ZHAIR), but now that I can, I still call them cheese puffs. This is the same basic recipe used to make cream puffs, but the addition of Parmesan cheese and ham makes them irresistibly salty and savory. Pipe the dough while it is still warm, or you won't get a good rise.* {MAKES 30 CHEESE PUFFS}

¼ cup whole milk

8 tablespoons (1 stick) unsalted butter, cut into tablespoons

1 teaspoon kosher salt

1 cup all-purpose flour

4 large eggs at room temperature, beaten

1½ cups (6 ounces) freshly grated Parmigiano-Reggiano cheese

⅓ cup (2 ounces) finely chopped smoked ham

2 tablespoons finely sliced fresh chives

¼ teaspoon freshly ground black pepper

⅛ teaspoon freshly grated nutmeg

Flaky sea salt, such as Maldon, for sprinkling

1. Position a rack in the center of the oven and preheat the oven to 375°F. Line a large rimmed baking sheet with parchment paper.

2. Combine ½ cup water with the milk in a heavy medium saucepan. Add the butter and kosher salt. Bring to a boil over medium heat, stirring often to help melt the butter. The butter must be completely melted by the time the liquid boils. Gradually stir in the flour to make a thick paste. Stir constantly until the dough forms a ball and the mixture films the bottom of the saucepan, about 1½ minutes.

3. Transfer the dough to a heatproof medium bowl. Let cool for 5 minutes. Using an electric mixer on medium speed, gradually beat in all but 1 tablespoon of the eggs in four or five additions, letting the first addition be absorbed before adding more. Reserve 1 tablespoon of the beaten eggs in the bowl. Beat 1¼ cups of the cheese, the ham, chives, pepper, and nutmeg into the dough.

4. Transfer the dough to a pastry bag fitted with a ½-inch-wide plain pastry tip. Pipe 30 mounds of dough, each about the size of a walnut and spaced about 1½ inches apart, onto the prepared baking sheet. Very lightly brush the tops of the mounds with the reserved beaten egg, using the brush to tamp down any pointed peaks of dough. Sprinkle the tops with the remaining ¼ cup of cheese. Sprinkle each puff very lightly with the sea salt.

5. Bake until the puffs have expanded and are golden brown, about 25 minutes. Do not underbake, or they will deflate when removed from the oven. Serve warm.

# Rustic Vegetable Soup

*contributed by* MICHAEL NORTHERN

*This is a heartwarming and soulful soup that is sure to delight those you serve it to. It doesn't take a lot of effort, even though it may look like a lot of ingredients—the soup comes together in one pot. For a vegetarian version, replace the chicken broth with vegetable broth. Use your very best olive oil to drizzle over each serving—this adds remarkable dimension to the taste and flavor.* {MAKES 8 SERVINGS}

3 tablespoons extra-virgin olive oil, plus more for drizzling

6 cloves garlic, minced

2 large shallots, chopped (about ½ cup)

¼ teaspoon red pepper flakes

1 yellow onion, chopped

1 tablespoon finely chopped fresh rosemary

1 tablespoon dried oregano

2 carrots, peeled and chopped

6 ounces cremini mushrooms, quartered

1 red bell pepper, seeded, deribbed, and cut into ½-inch dice

1 yellow bell pepper, seeded, deribbed, and cut into ½-inch dice

8 cups reduced-sodium chicken broth

1 can (28 ounces) peeled whole plum tomatoes, preferably San Marzano, crushed by hand, in juice (see Note, page 58)

2 cans (15 ounces each) cannellini beans, rinsed and drained

2 zucchini, cut into ¾-inch dice

1. Heat 3 tablespoons of olive oil in a heavy soup pot over medium heat. Add the garlic and cook, stirring occasionally, until fragrant, about 1 minute. Add the shallots and red pepper flakes and continue to cook, stirring often, until the shallots are translucent, about 1 minute.

2. Stir in the onion. Cook, stirring occasionally until softened, about 4 minutes. Stir in the rosemary and oregano and cook until fragrant, about 1 minute. Add the carrots, mushrooms, and bell peppers. Cook, stirring occasionally, until the carrots are softened, about 6 minutes.

3. Add the broth, tomatoes and their juices, beans, zucchini, and potatoes. Bring to a gentle boil. Reduce the heat to medium-low. Simmer until the potatoes are tender, about 35 minutes.

4. Remove the soup from the heat. Stir in the arugula and the ½ cup Parmigiano. Let stand until the arugula wilts, about 1 minute. Season with salt and pepper to taste.

5. Ladle into soup bowls and serve hot, with the olive oil for drizzling and extra Parmigiano passed on the side for guests to add to their soup as they wish.

*continued >*

4 small unpeeled Yukon Gold potatoes, cut into ¾-inch dice

3 cups (3 ounces) baby arugula

½ cup freshly grated Parmigiano-Reggiano, plus more for serving

Kosher salt

Freshly ground black pepper

↪ **NOTE:** To crush the tomatoes, pour them, with their juice, into a deep bowl. Squeeze and crush the tomatoes through your fingers (watch out for squirting juice) until the pieces are about the size of a dime.

# Hearty Oxtail Soup

*contributed by* IAN MACKINNON

*My grandmother used to make this delicious and comforting dish during the winter months. This is a great recipe to start early in the day and allow to braise and develop its flavors in the oven, filling the entire house with its aromas. The slow cooking allows the oxtails to literally melt into the broth for a full-bodied soup that will make it impossible for you to put down your spoon.* {MAKES 8 SERVINGS}

8 tablespoons olive oil

3 pounds oxtails, cut into 1-inch lengths

¼ cup all-purpose flour

Kosher salt

Freshly ground black pepper

2 yellow onions, cut into ½-inch dice

2 carrots, peeled and cut into ½-inch dice

2 celery stalks, cut into ½-inch dice

4 cloves garlic, minced

8 cups canned reduced-sodium beef broth

1 cup dry red wine

¼ cup tomato paste

2 tablespoons prepared horseradish

1 sprig fresh rosemary

1 sprig fresh thyme

1 bay leaf

2 green onions, including green parts chopped

1. Position a rack in the center of the oven; preheat oven to 350°F.

2. Pour 2 tablespoons of the olive oil into a large roasting pan. Bake until the oil is very hot, about 3 minutes. Meanwhile, sprinkle the oxtails with the flour, 1 tablespoon of salt, and 1 teaspoon of pepper, and toss to coat thoroughly. Remove the roasting pan from the oven. Shaking off the excess flour, place the oxtails in the pan and drizzle with 2 tablespoons of the olive oil. Return to the oven and bake until the oxtails are well browned, about 45 minutes.

3. While the oxtails are baking, heat the remaining 4 tablespoons oil in a large Dutch oven or ovenproof soup pot over medium heat. Add the onions, carrots, and celery. Cover and cook, stirring occasionally, until the onions are translucent, about 5 minutes. Stir in the garlic and cook until fragrant, about 1 minute.

4. Transfer the oxtails to the pot. Pour out any fat in the roasting pan. Heat the roasting pan over medium-high heat until it sizzles. Add 2 cups of the broth and bring to a boil, scraping up the browned bits in the bottom of the pan with a wooden spatula. Pour into the pot along with the remaining 6 cups of broth. Add the red wine, tomato paste, and horseradish and bring to a boil. Tie the rosemary, thyme, and bay leaf together with kitchen twine and add to the pot. Add water, if needed, to barely cover the ingredients.

5. Reduce the oven temperature to 300°F. Cover the pot with a close-fitting lid and transfer to the oven. Bake, stirring occasionally, until the meat is falling off the bones, about 3 hours. Remove the pot from the oven and skim off any fat that rises to the surface. Discard the herb bundle and as many bones as you can. Season to taste with salt and pepper. Ladle into soup bowls and serve, sprinkled with the green onions, reminding the diners to watch out for stray bones.

# Classic Clam Chowder

*contributed by* MICHAEL NORTHERN

*Clam chowder is another favorite soup that we serve at our restaurants. We tried many different versions and quickly established what makes great chowder. This one is neither too thick nor too thin, is flavorful, and is loaded with clams. Serve it with crusty bread or chowder crackers.*

{MAKES 8 TO 10 SERVINGS}

¾ cup (1½ sticks) unsalted butter

3 celery stalks, cut into ½-inch dice

1 yellow onion, cut into ½-inch dice

2 cloves garlic, minced

1½ teaspoons minced fresh thyme

½ teaspoon dried oregano

½ cup all-purpose flour

4⅔ cups whole milk

1⅓ cups heavy cream

1 large russet potato, peeled and cut into ½-inch dice

2 teaspoons Worcestershire sauce

½ teaspoon Tabasco sauce

1 bay leaf

2 cans (10 ounces each) baby clams, with their liquid

Kosher salt

Freshly ground black pepper

Chopped fresh flat-leaf parsley for garnish

1. Melt the butter in a soup pot over medium heat. Add the celery and onion and cook, stirring occasionally, until the onion is translucent, about 10 minutes. Stir in the garlic, thyme, and oregano and cook until the garlic is fragrant, about 2 minutes.

2. Reduce the heat to medium-low and sprinkle in the flour. Stir to coat the vegetables well. Cook, stirring occasionally, for about 4 minutes.

3. Slowly add the milk to the pot while stirring. The mixture will thicken and then thin out. Stir in the cream, diced potato, Worcestershire sauce, Tabasco, and bay leaf. Bring to a gentle simmer, stirring occasionally, over medium heat. Cook, stirring occasionally, until the potatoes are almost tender, about 10 minutes.

4. Reduce the heat to medium-low. Add the baby clams and their liquid to the pot. Simmer until the potatoes are tender, about 10 minutes more. Season the soup with salt and pepper. Remove the bay leaf. Ladle into soup bowls, sprinkle with parsley, and serve hot along with bread or crackers.

# MAIN-COURSE SALADS

# Grilled Chicken Salad with Strawberries and Goat Cheese

◆ *contributed by* TONY COLABELLI

*Nothing says spring like the appearance of local strawberries at the farmers' market or grocer's, and when they finally arrive, I serve them as much as possible. Take the grill out of hibernation and welcome the sweet berries (and the good weather) with a hearty salad featuring grilled chicken, along with sweet marinated onions, piquant goat cheese, and crunchy nuts.* {MAKES 6 SERVINGS}

**MARINATED RED ONIONS**

1 cup seasoned rice wine vinegar

⅓ cup sugar

1 teaspoon kosher salt

¼ teaspoon freshly ground black pepper

1 bay leaf

1 large red onion, cut into ¼-inch-thick half-moons

**DARK CHERRY BALSAMIC VINAIGRETTE**

½ cup balsamic vinegar

¼ cup sugar

½ cup cherry preserves

1 tablespoon mashed Simple Roasted Garlic (page 34)

¼ cup red wine vinegar

1 cup canola oil

Kosher salt

Freshly ground black pepper

1. To make the Marinated Red Onions, bring the vinegar, 1 cup water, sugar, salt, pepper, and bay leaf to a simmer in a medium nonreactive saucepan over high heat, stirring to dissolve the sugar and salt. Add the onion, return to a simmer, and cook for 1 minute. Remove from the heat. Transfer to a nonreactive bowl and let cool. Cover and refrigerate for at least 1 or up to 2 hours. Drain well, discarding the bay leaf. (The drained onions can be refrigerated in an airtight container for up to 4 days.)

2. To make the Dark Cherry Balsamic Vinaigrette, bring the balsamic vinegar and sugar to a simmer in a small nonreactive saucepan over medium heat, stirring frequently to dissolve the sugar. Simmer, uncovered, until the liquid is reduced by half, about 10 minutes. Add the cherry preserves and roasted garlic and cook 1 minute longer. Remove from the heat and let cool. Transfer to a blender, add the red wine vinegar, and purée until smooth. With the machine running, gradually add the canola oil in a steady stream. Season with salt and pepper.

3. Prepare a medium fire in a charcoal grill, or preheat a gas grill to medium (see Note, page 18).

1 pound boneless, skinless chicken
  breast halves, pounded to even
  thickness

2 tablespoons extra-virgin olive oil

Kosher salt

Freshly ground black pepper

8 ounces baby spinach

8 ounces mixed baby greens

2 pints fresh strawberries, hulled and
  cut into quarters

2 cups Baked Candied Pecans (page 30)
  or store-bought candied pecans

1 cup (4 ounces) crumbled rindless
  goat cheese (chèvre)

4. Brush the grill grate clean. Brush the chicken on both sides with the oil. Season the chicken with 1 teaspoon salt and ½ teaspoon pepper. Put on the grill and close the lid. Grill until the undersides are golden brown and seared with grill marks, about 4 minutes. Turn and grill until the chicken feels firm when pressed with a finger, about 4 minutes longer. Transfer to a cutting board and let cool. Cut the chicken crosswise, against the grain, into ¼-inch-thick slices. In batches, stack the pieces and cut crosswise into ¼-inch-wide strips. (The chicken can be prepared, cooled, covered, and refrigerated for up to 1 day.)

5. Toss the spinach and baby greens together in a large salad bowl. Add the chicken, marinated onions, half of the strawberries, and half of the candied pecans, and toss again to evenly distribute the ingredients. Drizzle with 1 cup of the vinaigrette and toss well. Season with salt and pepper. Divide the salad evenly among 6 chilled salad bowls or dinner plates, using tongs to heap the salad in a tall mound. Sprinkle with the goat cheese and remaining strawberries and candied pecans. Serve at once.

↪ NOTE: The recipe for the Dark Cherry Balsamic Vinaigrette makes about 2½ cups, although you'll need only 1 cup for this salad. Place the extra dressing in an airtight container for up to 1 month to use on other salads. Shake well before using.

# Wild Rice and Chicken Salad

*contributed by* SARELLE DROUGHT

*The serving possibilities for this refreshing salad are practically endless. It is terrific for carrying in your lunch box to work, or it can be turned into a sandwich or a wrap. One of my favorites is an open-faced sandwich of the salad on a baguette spread with stone-ground mustard and broiled with a topping of provolone cheese. Or, toss it with some mixed greens for a supper dish.*

{MAKES 6 SERVINGS}

Kosher salt

Freshly ground black pepper

1 pound boneless, skinless chicken breast halves

1 box (6 to 7 ounces) wild rice and long-grain rice blend with seasoning

3 ounces snow peas, trimmed and strings removed

⅓ cup seasoned rice wine vinegar

2 cloves garlic, minced

1 tablespoon Dijon mustard

½ teaspoon sugar

½ cup extra-virgin olive oil

4 green onions, including green parts, chopped

1 red bell pepper, seeded, deribbed, and cut into ½-inch dice

1 yellow bell pepper, seeded, deribbed, and cut into ½-inch dice

1 cup coarsely chopped Marcona almonds

1. Bring 6 cups water, 1 teaspoon salt, and ½ teaspoon pepper to a boil over high heat. Add the chicken breasts, stir once, and return to a boil. Immediately remove the pan from heat and cover it tightly with a lid. Let steep until the chicken shows no sign of pink when pierced in the thickest part, about 1 hour. Transfer to a plate and let cool until easy to handle. Chop the meat into bite-sized pieces. Transfer to a bowl, cover, and refrigerate.

2. Make the wild rice blend, with its seasoning packet, following the directions on the package. Transfer the rice to a bowl and let cool.

3. Bring a small saucepan of lightly salted water to a boil over high heat. Add the snow peas and cook just until they turn a brighter shade of green, about 1 minute. Drain in a sieve and rinse under cold running water until cooled. Pat dry with paper towels. Stack and cut the snow peas into quarters on a slight diagonal. Transfer to a bowl, cover, and refrigerate until serving.

4. Whisk the vinegar, garlic, mustard, sugar, ½ teaspoon salt, and ¼ teaspoon pepper together in a medium bowl. Gradually whisk in the oil.

5. Combine the chicken, rice mixture, green onions, and red and yellow peppers in a large bowl. Add half of the dressing and mix well. Cover and refrigerate for at least 30 minutes and up to 12 hours. Cover and refrigerate the remaining dressing.

6. Just before serving, add the almonds and snow peas to the chicken mixture. Add the remaining dressing and toss well. Season with salt and pepper. Serve chilled.

# Cilantro Lime Shrimp Salad

~ *contributed by* TONY COLABELLI

*This is another salad that, over time, has grown to become one of the most popular lunch offerings at our Bistro restaurants around the country. It has big Southwestern flavors that will wake up your palate. There is a real difference in flavor between wild and farmed shrimp, so for the best results, look for the former.* {MAKES 6 SERVINGS}

## CILANTRO LIME VINAIGRETTE

⅓ cup seasoned rice wine vinegar

¼ cup fresh lime juice

2 tablespoons honey

1 clove garlic, minced

1½ teaspoons minced canned chipotle chile in adobo

½ teaspoon kosher salt

¾ cup canola oil

1 cup tightly packed fresh cilantro leaves and stems

30 extra-large (16/20 count) shrimp, preferably wild caught, about 1⅔ pounds, peeled and deveined

¼ cup extra-virgin olive oil

3 cloves garlic, minced

Kosher salt

Freshly ground black pepper

3 ears corn, husked

1 pound mixed baby greens

2 cups (8 ounces) shredded Monterey Jack cheese

1. To make the Cilantro Lime Vinaigrette, combine the rice vinegar, lime juice, honey, garlic, chipotle, and salt in a blender or a food processor fitted with the metal blade. With the machine running, gradually add the canola oil. Add the cilantro and process until the vinaigrette is smooth.

2. Toss the shrimp with the olive oil, garlic, ¾ teaspoon salt, and ¼ teaspoon pepper in a shallow nonreactive dish. Cover and refrigerate while preparing the grill.

3. Prepare a hot fire in a charcoal grill, or preheat a gas grill to high (see Note, page 18). Brush the grill grate clean.

4. Put the corn on the grill and close the lid. Grill, turning occasionally, until the corn is hot and most of the kernels are deep brown, about 6 minutes. Transfer the corn to a platter and let cool until easy to handle.

5. Working with 1 ear at a time, stand it upright, stem end down, on a cutting board. Use a sharp knife to cut downward along the cob, removing the kernels and rotating the cob a quarter turn after each cut. Scoop the kernels into a bowl and discard the cob.

*continued >*

4 ripe plum (Roma) tomatoes, seeded
   and cut into ½-inch dice
   (about 2 cups)

1 large red bell pepper, roasted
   (see Notes), peeled, and cut into
   ½-inch dice

2 cups coarsely crushed tortilla chips

Cilantro sprigs for garnish

Lime wedges for serving

6. Drain the shrimp, discarding the oil. For a charcoal grill, the coals should have burned down to medium heat. (You should be able to hold your hand 1 inch above the grill grate for 3 seconds.) For a gas grill, adjust the heat to medium. Put the shrimp on the grill and close the lid. (If you wish, thread the shrimp on flat metal skewers, or use a metal grill screen to keep them from falling through the grate.) Cook until the edges of the shrimp are opaque, about 2 minutes. Turn the shrimp and continue grilling until opaque throughout, about 2 minutes more. Transfer to a plate.

7. Combine the greens, corn, Monterey Jack cheese, tomatoes, and roasted red pepper in a large bowl. Drizzle with 1 cup of the vinaigrette and toss. Season the salad with salt and pepper. Transfer the salad to 6 chilled salad bowls, building height in the center. Sprinkle each salad with some of the crushed tortilla chips. Arrange 5 grilled shrimp on each salad. Top with cilantro sprigs and garnish with lime wedges. Serve immediately.

🌿 NOTES: To roast bell pepper(s), prepare a hot fire in a charcoal grill, or preheat a gas grill to high (see Note, page 18). Brush the grill grate clean. (Or position a broiler rack about 8 inches from the source of heat and preheat the broiler.) Put the pepper(s) on the cooking grate (or broiler rack). Cover the grill and cook, turning occasionally, until blackened and blistered on all sides, 10 to 15 minutes. Transfer to a heatproof bowl and tightly cover with plastic wrap. Let stand for 15 minutes. Peel and remove the seeds and ribs from the pepper(s).

The recipe for Cilantro Lime Vinaigrette makes about 1½ cups, although you'll need only 1 cup for this recipe. Place the extra dressing in an airtight jar and refrigerate for up to 3 days to use on other salads. Shake well before using.

# Niçoise Salad with Salmon

~ *contributed by* MICHAEL NORTHERN

*If you order* salade niçoise *at a bistro in Nice, there may be variations on the basic theme of chunky seafood salad, but the fish is almost always canned tuna. In my version, a freshly roasted salmon fillet is the star, and it is so good you might make the salmon on its own as a dinner entrée.*

{MAKES 6 SERVINGS}

### DIJON BALSAMIC VINAIGRETTE

⅓ cup plus 1 tablespoon balsamic
vinegar

2 tablespoons minced red onion

2 tablespoons Dijon mustard

2 tablespoons packed brown sugar

½ teaspoon kosher salt

¼ teaspoon freshly ground black pepper

1 cup extra-virgin olive oil

1 tablespoon chopped fresh basil


6 ounces haricots verts or other thin
green beans, trimmed

### HERB-CRUSTED SALMON

3 green onions, including light green
parts, minced

3 tablespoons chopped fresh flat-leaf
parsley

3 tablespoons chopped fresh basil

2 teaspoons chopped fresh oregano

2 teaspoons chopped fresh thyme

2 large cloves garlic, minced

¼ cup extra-virgin olive oil

1. To make the Dijon Balsamic Vinaigrette, in a blender or in a food processor fitted with the metal blade, process the vinegar, onion, mustard, brown sugar, salt, and pepper until smooth. With the machine running, gradually add the olive oil in a thin, steady stream to form an emulsion. Add the basil and pulse to combine.

2. Bring a medium saucepan of lightly salted water to a boil over high heat. Add the green beans and cook until they are bright green and crisp-tender, about 2 minutes. Drain the beans in a colander and rinse under cold running water. Drain again and pat dry with paper towels.

3. To make the Herb-Crusted Salmon, position a rack in the center of the oven and preheat the oven to 450°F. Line a rimmed baking sheet with parchment paper. In a small bowl, mix the green onions, parsley, basil, oregano, thyme. and garlic together. Stir in the oil. Season the salmon on both sides with the salt and pepper. Place the salmon on the prepared baking sheet. Using a small rubber spatula or the back of a spoon, spread 1 teaspoon of the mustard over each fillet. Spread equal amounts of the herb mixture evenly over the fillets. Roast until the salmon is barely opaque when flaked with the tip of a knife, about 7 minutes.

*continued >*

Six 4-ounce salmon fillets, skin and pin
    bones removed

1 teaspoon kosher salt

½ teaspoon freshly ground black pepper

6 teaspoons Dijon mustard


1 pound mixed baby greens

12 ounces grape tomatoes, halved

½ cup pitted and halved Kalamata olives

3 tablespoons nonpareil capers, rinsed
    and drained

Kosher salt

Freshly ground black pepper

3½ cups Roasted Yukon Gold
    Potatoes (page 192), cooled
    to room temperature

18 to 24 thinly sliced red onion rings

6 hard-boiled eggs (see page 38),
    peeled and quartered

4. To assemble the salad, in a large bowl, place the greens, green beans, grape tomatoes, olives, and capers. Drizzle ¾ cup of the vinaigrette over the top and toss well. Season the salad with salt and pepper. Divide the salad among 6 chilled salad bowls. Top each with equal amounts of the potatoes and red onion rings. Arrange 4 egg quarters around the perimeter of each salad. Top each salad with a warm salmon fillet. Serve immediately.

↩ NOTE: The recipe for Dijon Balsamic Vinaigrette makes about 2 cups, although you'll need only ¾ cup for this recipe. Place the extra dressing in an airtight container and refrigerate for up to 3 days to use on other salads. Shake well before using.

# Grilled Shrimp, Corn, and Polenta Salad

*contributed by* TONY COLABELLI

*When creating a salad, it's all about balance—sweet and sour, crunchy and tender, and salty and savory flavors and textures come into play. Here's a salad that has it all, with summery corn and spicy arugula, crispy Parmesan cheese and sweet shrimp.* {MAKES 6 SERVINGS}

**PARMESAN CRISPS**

1 cup (4 ounces) freshly grated
  Parmigiano-Reggiano cheese

**CREAMY GARLIC DRESSING**

¼ cup Champagne or white wine
  vinegar

3 tablespoons mayonnaise

1 green onion, white and green parts,
  minced

1 tablespoon plus 1½ teaspoons honey

1 tablespoon mashed Simple Roasted
  Garlic (page 34)

2 teaspoons Dijon mustard

1 small clove garlic, minced

1 teaspoon fresh lemon juice

1 teaspoon chopped fresh dill

1 teaspoon chopped fresh flat-leaf parsley

1 teaspoon kosher salt

¼ teaspoon freshly ground black pepper

1 cup canola oil

1. To make the Parmesan Crisps, heat a large nonstick pan over medium heat. Line 2 baking sheets with parchment paper. Sprinkle ¼ cup of the cheese in an even layer in the pan and cook until the edges turn golden brown, about 1½ minutes. Use a heatproof spatula to transfer the crisp to a prepared baking sheet and let cool. Repeat to make three more crisps. Coarsely crumble the crisps.

2. To make the Creamy Garlic Dressing, combine the vinegar, mayonnaise, green onion, honey, roasted garlic, Dijon mustard, garlic, lemon juice, dill, parsley, salt, and pepper in a blender or food processor fitted with the metal blade. With the machine running, gradually add the oil in a thin, steady stream to form an emulsion.

3. Prepare a hot fire in a charcoal grill, or preheat a gas grill to high (see Note, page 18).

4. Brush the grill grate clean. Put the corn on the grill and close the lid. Grill, turning occasionally, until the corn is hot and the kernels are golden brown, about 6 minutes. Transfer the corn to a platter and let cool until easy to handle.

5. While the corn is cooling, lightly brush the polenta slices with olive oil. Add to the grill and cook, turning once, until seared with grill marks, about 2½ minutes per side. Transfer to a plate and let cool.

6. Working with 1 ear at a time, stand it upright, stem end down, on a cutting board. Use a sharp knife to cut downward along the cob, removing the kernels and rotating the cob a quarter turn after each cut. Scoop the kernels into a bowl and discard the cob.

3 ears corn, husked

1 log (1 pound) store-bought polenta,
   cut into ¾-inch-thick rounds

¼ cup extra-virgin olive oil, plus more
   for brushing

30 extra-large (16/20 count) shrimp,
   preferably wild caught, about 1⅔
   pounds, peeled and deveined

2 cloves garlic, very finely minced

Kosher salt

Freshly ground black pepper

1 pound baby arugula

1 pint cherry or grape tomatoes, halved

7. Meanwhile, toss the shrimp with the ¼ cup olive oil and minced garlic in a shallow nonreactive dish. Season with salt and pepper. For a charcoal grill, the coals should have burned down to medium heat. (You should be able to hold your hand 1 inch above the grill grate for 3 seconds.) For a gas grill, adjust the heat to medium.

8. Drain the shrimp, discarding the marinade. Put the shrimp on the grill and cover. (A metal grill screen or flat-bladed metal skewers are helpful to keep the shrimp from falling through the grate.) Grill until the edges are opaque, about 2 minutes. Turn the shrimp and continue grilling until opaque throughout, about 2 minutes more. Transfer to a plate.

9. Cut the grilled polenta into ¾-inch cubes. Combine the arugula, tomatoes, and corn in a large bowl. Drizzle with 1 cup of the dressing and toss. Add the Parmesan crisps and toss again. Season with salt and pepper. Transfer to 6 chilled salad bowls. Divide the shrimp and polenta cubes equally among the salads. Serve immediately.

↬ NOTE: The recipe for Creamy Garlic Dressing makes about 1½ cups, although you'll need only 1 cup for this recipe. The dressing can be refrigerated in an airtight container for up to 5 days and used on other salads. Shake well before using.

# Chopped Vegetable Salad with Sherry Vinaigrette

~ *contributed by* MICHAEL NORTHERN

*From the first day that our Blue Stove Restaurant opened, this confetti-colored salad has been featured on the menu. These are the vegetables that we typically use, but feel free to exchange others—whatever you like or find at the market in their freshest, most vibrant state. The quality of the sherry vinegar is critical to the recipe's success, so splurge on a top brand at a gourmet shop.* {MAKES 6 SERVINGS}

## SHERRY MUSTARD VINAIGRETTE

½ cup plus 1 tablespoon extra-virgin olive oil

3 tablespoons minced shallots

1 tablespoon minced garlic

½ cup aged sherry vinegar

1 tablespoon Dijon mustard

½ teaspoon kosher salt

⅛ teaspoon freshly ground white pepper

¼ cup almond oil or extra-virgin olive oil


2 carrots, peeled and cut into ¼-inch dice

1½ cups fresh corn kernels (from about 3 ears)

6 ounces haricots verts or other thin green beans, trimmed

10 ounces mixed baby greens

3 celery stalks, cut into ¼-inch dice

½ small jicama, peeled and cut into ¼-inch dice (about 1½ cups)

2 large yellow bell peppers, seeded, deribbed, and cut into ¼-inch dice

1. To make the Sherry Mustard Vinaigrette, heat 1 tablespoon of the oil in a small skillet over low heat. Add the shallots and garlic and cook, stirring often, until golden, about 5 minutes. Remove from heat and stir in the vinegar, mustard, salt, and pepper. Let cool. Transfer to a blender or a food processor fitted with the metal blade. With the machine running, gradually add the remaining ½ cup of olive oil and the almond oil and process until smooth.

2. Bring a large saucepan of lightly salted water to a boil over high heat. Add the carrots and cook until crisp-tender, about 4 minutes. Use a wire-mesh skimmer to scoop the carrots out of the water, and transfer them to a large bowl of ice water.

3. Add the corn to the boiling water and cook just until tender, about 2 minutes. Use the skimmer to transfer the corn to the bowl with the carrots. Let the corn stand for 3 minutes to cool. Drain the vegetables in a colander. Pat dry with paper towels and put in a large bowl.

4. Add the green beans to the boiling water and cook until crisp-tender, about 2 minutes. Drain in a colander and rinse under cold running water to stop the cooking. Chop the green beans into ¼-inch lengths. Pat dry with paper towels and add to the bowl with the carrots and corn.

*continued >*

6 ripe plum (Roma) tomatoes, seeded and cut into ¼-inch dice

5 green onions, including pale green parts, thinly sliced

Kosher salt

Freshly ground black pepper

¼ cup freshly grated Parmigiano-Reggiano for serving

2 tablespoons finely chopped fresh chives for serving

5. In another large bowl, place the mixed greens. Drizzle with ¼ cup of the vinaigrette, season with salt and pepper, and toss to coat evenly. Divide equally among 6 chilled deep soup bowls or dinner plates, creating nests for the vegetable mixture.

6. Add the celery, jicama, bell peppers, tomatoes, and green onions to the corn mixture. Add ¾ cup of the vinaigrette and mix well. Season the salad with salt and pepper.

7. Divide the vegetable mixture evenly among the salads, spooning it into the center of the greens in each bowl. Sprinkle with equal amounts of Parmigiano and chives. Serve immediately.

↝ NOTE: The recipe for Sherry Mustard Vinaigrette makes about 1½ cups, although you'll need only 1 cup for this recipe. The dressing can be refrigerated in an airtight container for up to 3 days to use on other salads. Shake well before using.

# Berry Salad with Vanilla Bean Vinaigrette

↜ *contributed by* KIMBERLY HAZARD

*Served in a large bowl, this colorful, sassy mix of sweet, tart, and savory is an excellent choice for a warm-weather brunch buffet. It is also a delicious option for a light lunch, and the perfect showcase for local berries, such as huckleberries, marionberries, or wild blueberries.* {MAKES 6 TO 8 SERVINGS}

VANILLA BEAN VINAIGRETTE

3 tablespoons Champagne or white wine vinegar

2 teaspoons sugar

1½ teaspoons Dijon mustard

2 teaspoons finely minced shallot

¼ teaspoon finely minced garlic

1 vanilla bean

⅔ cup canola oil

Kosher salt

Freshly ground white pepper

8 ounces mixed baby greens

8 ounces baby spinach

2 cups fresh strawberries, hulled and quartered

2 cups fresh blueberries

1 cup fresh raspberries

¾ cup (3 ounces) pistachios, toasted (see Note) and coarsely chopped

Kosher salt

Freshly ground black pepper

1 cup (4 ounces) crumbled rindless goat cheese (chèvre)

1. To make the Vanilla Bean Vinaigrette, whisk the vinegar, sugar, mustard, shallot, and garlic in a medium bowl. Split the vanilla bean in half lengthwise. Use the tip of a knife to scrape the tiny seeds from the pod halves into the bowl. (Save the pod halves for another use.) Gradually whisk in the oil. Season with salt and white pepper. (The vinaigrette can be refrigerated in an airtight container for up to 1 day. Shake well before using.)

2. Toss the baby greens and spinach in a large bowl. Drizzle with the vinaigrette and add half the strawberries, blueberries, raspberries, and pistachios. Toss gently and season with salt and pepper.

3. Divide the salad evenly among 6 chilled salad bowls or dinner plates, shaping each into a mound. Scatter equal amounts of the remaining strawberries, blueberries, raspberries, and pistachios over each, then top with the goat cheese. Serve immediately.

↜ NOTE: To toast pistachios, spread the nuts on a rimmed baking sheet. Bake in a preheated 350°F oven, stirring occasionally, until fragrant and lightly toasted, about 10 minutes. Let cool completely before chopping.

# Fresh Berry and Balsamic Fig Salad with Goat Cheese

*contributed by* KIMBERLY HAZARD

*I was lucky enough to live and cook in Modena, Italy, birthplace of balsamic vinegar, where I learned a lot about the foods that work best with this sweet, thick condiment. Berries and figs are two such ingredients, and both are featured in this elegant fruit salad.* {MAKES 6 SERVINGS}

**BALSAMIC FIG VINAIGRETTE**

½ cup (1½ ounces) coarsely chopped dried Mission figs

¼ cup balsamic vinegar

2 tablespoons sugar

¼ cup cherry preserves

1½ teaspoons mashed Simple Roasted Garlic (page 34)

3 tablespoons red wine vinegar

½ teaspoon kosher salt

¼ teaspoon freshly ground black pepper

½ cup canola oil

10 ounces mixed baby greens

6 ounces baby arugula

15 dried Mission figs, cut lengthwise into quarters

1 cup Spiced Whole Almonds (page 31)

2 cups fresh strawberries, hulled and quartered

1½ cups fresh blueberries

Kosher salt

Freshly ground black pepper

1. To make the Balsamic Fig Vinaigrette, bring the figs, balsamic vinegar, and sugar to a simmer in a small nonreactive saucepan over medium heat, stirring frequently to dissolve the sugar. Simmer, uncovered, until the liquid is reduced by half, about 10 minutes. Add the cherry preserves and roasted garlic and cook for 1 minute longer. Let cool. Transfer the mixture to a blender or food processor fitted with the metal blade. Add the red wine vinegar, salt, and pepper. Process until the figs are finely chopped. With the machine running, add the oil in a thin, steady stream to form an emulsion. One table-spoon at a time, add 3 tablespoons of water.

2. Combine the mixed greens and arugula in a large bowl. Add the figs and the almonds, drizzle with 1 cup of the vinaigrette and toss. Add the strawberries and blueberries and toss again. Season with salt and pepper.

3. Divide the salad evenly among 6 chilled salad bowls. Scatter equal amounts of the goat cheese, raspberries, and blackberries evenly over the salads. Serve immediately.

*continued >*

1½ cups (6 ounces) crumbled rindless
  goat cheese (chèvre)

1½ cups fresh raspberries

1½ cups fresh blackberries

**NOTE:** The recipe for Balsamic Fig Vinaigrette makes about 1½ cups, although only 1 cup is needed for this recipe. Place the extra vinaigrette in an airtight container in the refrigerator for up to 3 days to use on other salads. Shake well before using.

# Iceberg Wedge Salad with Blue Cheese and Bacon

*contributed by* MICHAEL NORTHERN

*Iceberg lettuce deserves more respect. Refreshingly crisp and sturdy, it can hold up under this classic blue cheese dressing to make one of the all-time great American salads.* {MAKES 4 SERVINGS}

**BLUE CHEESE DRESSING**

1 tablespoon distilled white vinegar

½ teaspoon dry mustard

1 cup mayonnaise

¼ cup sour cream

1 teaspoon Worcestershire sauce

Dash of Tabasco sauce

½ clove garlic, minced

¼ teaspoon kosher salt

Pinch of freshly ground white pepper

⅓ cup (about 1½ ounces) crumbled blue cheese

8 ounces thick-sliced bacon

1 head iceberg lettuce, cored, quartered, and quarters halved crosswise to make 8 pieces

3 plum (Roma) tomatoes, cored and quartered

Kosher salt

Freshly ground black pepper

20 thinly sliced red onion rings

1 cup (4 ounces) crumbled blue cheese

1½ cups Baked Candied Pecans (page 30)

1. To make the Blue Cheese Dressing, in a small bowl, whisk 1 tablespoon water with the vinegar and dry mustard to dissolve the mustard. Add the mayonnaise, sour cream, Worcestershire, Tabasco, garlic, salt, and white pepper and whisk to combine. Add the blue cheese and whisk again. Cover and refrigerate for at least 1 hour to blend the flavors. (The dressing can be refrigerated in an airtight container for up to 3 days. Stir well before using.)

2. In a large skillet, cook the bacon over medium heat, turning occasionally, until crisp and browned, about 10 minutes. Transfer to paper towels and let cool. Chop into ½-inch dice.

3. For each serving, place 2 tablespoons dressing in the center of each of 4 dinner plates. Place a wedge of lettuce, cut side down, on top of the dressing on each plate. Lean a second wedge across the first wedge.

4. Divide the remaining dressing evenly over the salads, carefully masking about a third of the lettuce with the dressing.

5. Season the tomatoes with salt and pepper. Evenly space 3 wedges, cut sides up, around the perimeter of each salad. Arrange equal amounts of the onion rings on the salads. Evenly divide equal amounts of the chopped bacon and scatter the blue cheese crumbles over the salads, and top with the pecans. Grind fresh pepper over each, if desired, and serve immediately.

# BEEF, PORK, LAMB & VEAL

# Skirt Steak with Romesco Sauce and Balsamic Roast Onions

✂ *contributed by* MICHAEL LYLE

*To my taste, thanks to its generous marbling, skirt steak is by far the most flavorful cut of beef. I often grill it outside, but it is also terrific cooked in a skillet, where it develops a savory crust. As this version is served with romesco, the Spanish red pepper sauce, a bottle of red Rioja would be in order.* {MAKES 4 SERVINGS}

## BALSAMIC ROAST ONIONS

½ cup balsamic vinegar

¼ cup honey

2 tablespoons extra-virgin olive oil

2 teaspoons chopped fresh thyme

1 large red onion, cut into ½-inch-thick rings

Kosher salt

Freshly ground black pepper

## ROMESCO SAUCE

1 cup (4 ounces) blanched slivered almonds, toasted (see Note, page 88)

2 red bell peppers, roasted (see Note, page 70), seeded, and chopped

3 tablespoons extra-virgin olive oil, or as needed

¼ teaspoon ground cumin

Kosher salt

Freshly ground black pepper

1. To make the Balsamic Roast Onions, preheat the oven to 350°F. Line a rimmed baking sheet with parchment paper.

2. In a medium bowl, whisk the balsamic vinegar, honey, oil, and thyme together. Arrange the onion slices on the prepared baking sheet, season with salt and pepper, and evenly pour the vinegar mixture over the onion. Bake, stirring occasionally, until the onions are tender and the vinegar mixture has thickened, about 30 minutes. Let cool on the baking sheet. Transfer the onions and pan juices to a bowl. (The onions can be covered and refrigerated for up to 2 days. Let come to room temperature before serving.)

3. To make the Romesco Sauce, pulse the almonds in a food processor fitted with the metal blade until coarsely chopped. Add the roasted peppers, the 3 tablespoons oil, and the cumin and process, adding more oil through the processor feed tube as needed until the mixture resembles thick pesto. Transfer to a bowl and season with salt and pepper. (The romesco sauce can be refrigerated in an airtight container for up to 2 days. Let come to room temperature before serving. Add more olive oil to adjust the thickness and reseason with salt and pepper.)

*continued >*

4 skirt steaks (about 6 ounces each)

1½ teaspoons kosher salt

½ teaspoon freshly ground black pepper

2 teaspoons canola oil

Chopped fresh chives for garnish

4. Season the skirt steaks with the salt and pepper and let stand at room temperature for 30 minutes. Add the oil to a very large, heavy skillet (preferably cast iron) and heat over medium heat until very hot. Add the steaks and cook until the undersides are well browned, about 3 minutes. (Be sure your range vent is on high, or open a kitchen window.) Flip the steaks over and continue cooking until the other sides are well browned and a steak feels only slightly resilient when the center is pressed with a finger, about 3 minutes more. Transfer to a carving board and let stand for 5 minutes.

5. Using a spatula, divide the romesco sauce among 4 dinner plates, mounding the sauce in a 6-inch strip in the center of each plate. Use a sharp knife to cut each steak crosswise on the diagonal across the grain into 6 equal pieces. Transfer each steak to a plate, arranging the slices over the romesco sauce. Top each steak with equal amounts of the roasted onion and drizzle with the carving juices from the board. Sprinkle with the chives. Serve hot.

↩ NOTE: To toast the almonds, spread them on a rimmed baking sheet. Bake in a preheated 325°F oven, stirring occasionally, until toasted and fragrant, about 8 minutes. Let cool completely.

# Grilled Rib-Eye Steaks with Chipotle Lime Butter

*contributed by* ROB GIBBS

*Ever since I began cooking professionally, I have counted on my younger brother, Ryan, as a reliable taste-tester. (He's not so little anymore, but I still think of him as my "little brother.") I created this dish with his favorite big flavors in gratitude for his honest critiques, both good and bad, over the years. These steaks are now served at all of the Gibbs family barbecues with mounds of homemade potato salad.* {MAKES 4 SERVINGS}

### CHIPOTLE LIME BUTTER

½ cup (1 stick) unsalted butter, at room temperature

Grated zest of ½ lime

1 tablespoon fresh lime juice

1 canned chipotle chile in adobo, minced

1 teaspoon adobo sauce from canned chipotle chiles in adobo

½ teaspoon ground cumin

Kosher salt

Freshly ground black pepper

### STEAK SEASONING

1 tablespoon kosher salt

1 teaspoon granulated garlic

1 teaspoon onion powder

½ teaspoon freshly ground black pepper

½ teaspoon sweet paprika

Large pinch of cayenne pepper

Four 1-pound rib-eye steaks on the bone, cut about 1¼ inches thick

1. To make the Chipotle Lime Butter, mash the butter, lime zest and juice, chipotle, adobo sauce, and cumin together in a small bowl with a rubber spatula. Season with salt and pepper. Transfer to a sheet of plastic wrap. Use the plastic to shape the butter into a thick log. Twist the ends of the wrap in opposite directions to tighten the roll. Put on a plate and refrigerate until firm, about 3 hours.

2. To make the Steak Seasoning, mix the salt, granulated garlic, onion powder, pepper, paprika, and cayenne together in a small bowl. Sprinkle the seasoning on both sides of the steaks. Let stand at room temperature for 30 minutes.

3. Prepare a hot fire in a charcoal grill, or preheat a gas grill to high (see Note, page 18).

4. Brush the grill grate clean. Lightly oil the grate. Place the steaks on the grill and close the lid. Cook until the undersides are seared with grill marks, about 2 minutes. Rotate the steaks 90 degrees, then cook for 2 minutes more. Flip the steaks and continue grilling, rotating the steaks after 2 minutes, until they feel barely resilient when pressed in the center with a fingertip, 3 to 5 minutes longer for medium-rare. If flare-ups occur, move the steaks to a cooler area of the grill (that is, the perimeter of the grate on a charcoal grill, or over a turned-off burner of a gas grill).

5. Transfer each steak to a plate. Slice the butter into 8 equal rounds. Top each steak with 2 butter rounds and serve, letting the butter melt over the steak.

# Steak al Forno

*～ contributed by* MICHAEL NORTHERN

*I learned this dish many years ago during my first stint in a professional kitchen. The steaks are grilled to give them that ineffable charcoal flavor, and then finished under the broiler with Parmigiano, parsley, and garlic butter to create a golden brown crust.* {MAKES 4 SERVINGS}

4 top loin steaks (also called New York or strip steaks), each about 1 pound and 1½ inches thick

1½ cups (6 ounces) freshly grated Parmigiano-Reggiano cheese

2 tablespoons minced fresh flat-leaf parsley

4 tablespoons (½ stick) unsalted butter

2 cloves garlic, minced

1 tablespoon kosher salt

1 teaspoon freshly ground black pepper

1. Prepare a hot fire in a charcoal grill, or preheat a gas grill on high (see Note, page 18).

2. Let the steaks stand at room temperature while heating the grill. Mix the Parmigiano and parsley in a small bowl, being sure to combine them well. Set the Parmigiano mixture aside.

3. Cook the butter and garlic together in a small saucepan over medium-low heat until the butter is bubbling and the garlic is lightly cooked, about 1 minute. Set the garlic butter aside.

4. Pat the steaks dry with paper towels. Season them with the salt and pepper. Position the broiler rack about 8 inches from the heat source and preheat the broiler on high. Line a rimmed baking sheet with aluminum foil.

5. Brush the grill grate clean. Lightly oil the grate. Place the steaks on the grill and close the lid. Grill until the undersides are seared with grill marks, about 2 minutes. Rotate the steaks 90 degrees, then cook for 2 minutes more. Flip the steaks, cover, and continue grilling, rotating the steaks after 2 minutes, until the steaks feel barely resilient when pressed in the center with a fingertip, 3 to 5 minutes longer for medium-rare. If flare-ups occur, move the steaks to a cooler area of the grill (that is, the perimeter of the grate on a charcoal grill, or a turned-off burner of a gas grill).

6. Transfer the steaks to the prepared baking sheet. Divide the Parmigiano mixture evenly over the steaks and press gently onto the steaks to adhere. Drizzle the garlic butter evenly over the cheese covering the steaks. Broil until the cheese is melted and beginning to turn golden brown, 1 to 2 minutes. Let stand for 3 minutes before serving.

# Sixth & Pine Meatloaf

*contributed by* MICHAEL LYLE

*At Sixth & Pine, our casual restaurants featuring home-style cooking, we serve this meatloaf with pride. A delicate balance of earthy herbs, smoky bacon, and savory cheese gives it a blue ribbon. Any leftovers make a perfect sandwich, served on a toasted bun with ketchup and melted Cheddar cheese.* {MAKES 6 SERVINGS}

3 slices thick-sliced bacon, coarsely chopped

2 tablespoons extra-virgin olive oil

1 yellow onion, cut into ¼-inch dice

2 teaspoons finely chopped fresh rosemary

1 teaspoon finely chopped fresh thyme

½ cup dried plain bread crumbs

½ cup whole milk

2 pounds ground round (85 percent lean)

½ cup freshly grated Parmigiano-Reggiano cheese

2 large eggs, beaten

1 tablespoon kosher salt

½ teaspoon freshly ground black pepper

1. Position a rack in the center of the oven and preheat the oven to 350°F. Line a rimmed baking sheet with parchment paper.

2. Cook the bacon in a medium skillet over medium-high heat, stirring occasionally, until crisp and browned, about 10 minutes. Use a slotted spoon to transfer to paper towels to drain. Pour out the fat.

3. Add the oil to the skillet and heat over medium heat. Add the onion and cook, stirring occasionally, until translucent, about 5 minutes. Reduce the heat to low. Stir in the rosemary and thyme and cook to release their aromas, about 2 minutes. Transfer to a large bowl. Add the bread crumbs and milk and let stand until the milk is absorbed, about 3 minutes. Add the ground round, cooked bacon, Parmigiano, eggs, salt, and pepper. Mix until combined (your cleaned hands work well). Transfer to the baking sheet and shape into an oval-shaped loaf about 12 inches long and 4½ inches wide.

4. Bake until browned and an instant-read thermometer inserted in the center of the loaf reads 150°F, about 1 hour. Let cool on the baking sheet for 5 minutes. Use a wide spatula to transfer the loaf to a platter. Slice and serve.

# Beef Bourguignon

*contributed by* JONATHAN ROHLAND

*There are no shortcuts to making this classic beef stew. If you can stand the wait, try refrigerating it for a day or two before serving, and you'll find that the flavors will mingle even more. It goes without saying to serve the ragout over noodles, mashed potatoes, or rice so not a single drop of the red wine sauce goes to waste.* {MAKES 8 SERVINGS}

**BOUQUET GARNI**

4 sprigs fresh rosemary, each about
   3 inches long

4 sprigs fresh thyme, each about
   3 inches long

1 teaspoon black peppercorns

3 bay leaves

8 ounces white pearl onions

4 tablespoons extra-virgin olive oil

8 ounces slab bacon, rind removed,
   cut into ¼-inch dice

4 pounds boneless beef chuck, cut into
   1½-inch pieces

1 tablespoon kosher salt

1 teaspoon freshly ground black pepper

6 cloves garlic, minced

1 bottle (750 ml) Pinot Noir

2 cups reduced-sodium beef broth

1 tablespoon tomato paste

3 carrots, peeled and cut into
   ½-inch dice

4 tablespoons (½ stick) unsalted butter

¼ cup all-purpose flour

1 pound cremini mushrooms, quartered

Chopped fresh flat-leaf parsley
   for garnish

1. Position a rack in the center of the oven and preheat the oven to 300°F.

2. To make the Bouquet Garni, rinse a 12-inch square piece of cheese-cloth in water and wring it out. Wrap the rosemary, thyme, pepper-corns, and bay leaves in the cheesecloth and tie into a packet with kitchen string.

3. Bring a small saucepan of water to a boil over high heat. Add the pearl onions and boil until the skins loosen, about 2 minutes. Drain and rinse under cold running water. Use a sharp paring knife to trim off the tops and tails; peel the onions. Pierce each with the tip of the knife to help hold its shape during cooking.

4. Heat 2 tablespoons of the oil in a large Dutch oven over medium heat. Add the bacon and cook, stirring occasionally, until browned, about 10 minutes. Use a slotted spoon to transfer the bacon to a platter, reserving the fat in the Dutch oven.

5. Season the beef with the salt and pepper. Increase the heat to medium-high. Working in batches to avoid crowding, add the beef and cook, turning occasionally, until browned on all sides, about 8 minutes. Use the slotted spoon to transfer the beef to the platter with the bacon.

*continued >*

6. Return the heat to medium. Add the onions and cook, stirring occasionally, until golden brown, about 6 minutes. Stir in the garlic and cook until fragrant, about 1 minute. Add the wine and bring to a boil, scraping up the browned bits in the pot bottom with a wooden spatula. Stir in the broth and tomato paste and add the bouquet garni. Return the beef and bacon to the pot and add the carrots. Return to a boil. Cover the pot with aluminum foil, and then cover with the lid.

7. Bake until the meat is very tender when pierced with a fork, about 2 hours. Remove from the oven and skim off any fat from the surface of the cooking liquid. Discard the bouquet garni. Put the Dutch oven on the stove over medium-low heat.

8. Melt the butter in a medium saucepan over medium-low heat. Whisk in the flour and let bubble without browning for 1 minute. Remove from the heat and whisk in about 1½ cups of the cooking liquid. Stir this mixture into the stew. Simmer, uncovered, until the sauce thickens and no raw flour taste remains, about 15 minutes.

9. Meanwhile, heat the remaining 2 tablespoons of oil in a large skillet over medium-high heat until hot but not smoking. Add the mushrooms and cook, stirring occasionally, until their liquid has evaporated and they are sizzling and browned, about 10 minutes. Stir into the stew. Taste and adjust the seasoning. Serve hot, sprinkled with the parsley. (The stew can be cooled, covered, and refrigerated, for up to 3 days, or frozen for up to 3 months. Reheat over medium-low heat before serving.)

# Grilled Skirt Steak with Cilantro Lime Vinaigrette

*contributed by* MICHAEL LYLE

*Our popular Cilantro Lime Vinaigrette (page 69) goes beyond the salad bowl to become a sauce for grilled skirt steak, a marbled cut that benefits from the acidic vinaigrette to cut its richness. This almost ridiculously simple dish is terrific accompanied by the Roasted Yukon Gold Potatoes and Asparagus on page 192.* {MAKES 6 SERVINGS}

6 skirt steaks, about 6 ounces each

2 teaspoons kosher salt

½ teaspoon freshly ground black pepper

¾ cup Cilantro Lime Vinaigrette (page 69)

1. Season the steaks with salt and pepper. Let stand at room temperature while preparing the grill.

2. Prepare a hot fire in a charcoal grill, or preheat a gas grill on high (see Note, page 18).

3. Brush the grill grate clean. Lightly oil the grate. Place the steaks on the grill and close the lid. Cook, with the lid closed as much as possible, until the undersides are browned, about 3 minutes. Flip the steaks, and cook until the steaks feel barely resilient when pressed with a fingertip, about 3 minutes more. Transfer the steaks to a carving board and let rest about 5 minutes.

4. With the knife held at a 45-degree angle, cut the steak into thin slices. Arrange each sliced steak on a dinner plate. Drizzle a little of the vinaigrette over each steak and serve, with the remaining vinaigrette passed on the side.

# Short Ribs Provençal

↜ contributed by MICHAEL LEPAGE

*There is nothing wrong with all-American beef stew, slowly simmered to tenderness with vegetables and served on a bed of noodles. But the French often use short ribs, whose bones give even more flavor to the sauce, and season the stew with the aromatic blend herbes de Provence, which can now be found at most supermarkets.* {MAKES 6 SERVINGS}

5 pounds individual (not cross-cut) bone-in beef short ribs, trimmed of excess fat

Kosher salt

Freshly ground black pepper

4 tablespoons extra-virgin olive oil

1 large yellow onion, chopped

2 carrots, peeled and cut into ½-inch dice

2 celery stalks, cut into ½-inch dice

8 cloves garlic, minced

1 can (15.5 ounces) diced tomatoes in juice

2 teaspoons herbes de Provence

1 cup dry red wine

4 cups reduced-sodium beef broth

2 bay leaves

1 cup pitted and coarsely chopped Kalamata olives

3 tablespoons cold unsalted butter, cut into tablespoons

Chopped fresh flat-leaf parsley for garnish

Hot cooked noodles for serving

1. Preheat the oven to 300°F.

2. Season the ribs with 1 tablespoon salt and 2 teaspoons pepper. Heat 2 tablespoons of the oil in a large Dutch oven over medium-high heat. Working in batches to avoid crowding, add the short ribs and cook, turning occasionally, until browned on all sides, about 5 minutes. Transfer the short ribs to a plate.

3. Add the remaining 2 tablespoons of oil to the pot and lower the pot to medium-low heat. Add the onion, carrots, celery, and garlic and cook, stirring occasionally, until the onion is translucent, about 5 minutes. Add the tomatoes along with their juices and the herbes de Provence. Bring to a boil over high heat and cook until the juices evaporate slightly, about 3 minutes. Add the wine, scraping up the browned bits on the pot bottom with a wooden spatula, and boil for 1 minute. Stir in the broth and bay leaves.

4. Return the short ribs to the pot and bring the liquid to a boil. Cover tightly. Bake until the short ribs are very tender when pierced with the tip of a sharp knife, about 2½ hours. Using kitchen tongs, transfer the ribs to a warmed deep platter and remove the bay leaves. Cover the platter with aluminum foil to keep warm.

5. Skim the fat from the surface of the cooking liquid. Return the pot to high heat and bring to a boil. Cook, stirring often, until the liquid has reduced by half, about 15 minutes. Skim off any fat or foam that rises to the surface. Add the olives and cook for 1 minute. Remove from the heat. One tablespoon at a time, stir in the butter until it is incorporated. Season with salt and pepper. Pour the sauce over the short ribs and sprinkle with the parsley. Serve immediately, with the noodles.

# Blue Cheese Sirloin Burgers

*contributed by* MICHAEL THOMS

*Anyone can toss some thawed preshaped patties on the grill, but these burgers are thick pucks of ground sirloin (when I am feeling flush, I use Japanese wagyu, the most premium beef on the market, or you might want to opt for grass-fed beef), filled with sharp blue cheese. Don't overdo the condiments, so the burgers' flavors can shine through.* {MAKES 4 SERVINGS}

2 pounds top-quality ground sirloin (90 percent lean)

6 ounces blue cheese, preferably Roquefort or Gorgonzola, coarsely crumbled

2 teaspoons kosher salt

½ teaspoon freshly ground black pepper

4 sandwich rolls, preferably brioche, split

8 ripe tomato slices

4 large leaves Bibb lettuce

Tomato ketchup, Sriracha Aïoli (page 129), and Dijon mustard

1. Divide the beef into 8 equal portions and flatten each into a 5-inch-diameter patty. For each burger, top a patty with one-quarter of the blue cheese, leaving a ¾-inch border. Top with another patty and thoroughly seal the edges. Mix the salt and pepper together. Season the burgers on both sides with the salt and pepper mixture. Set aside at room temperature while preparing the grill.

2. Prepare a medium fire in a charcoal grill, or preheat a gas grill on medium (see Note, page 18).

3. Brush the grill grate clean. Lightly oil the grate. Put the burgers on the grill and close the lid. Cook until the underside is well browned, about 3 minutes. Flip the burgers and continue grilling until the other sides are browned and the beef feels barely resilient when pressed in the center with a fingertip, about 3 minutes for medium-rare. If flare-ups occur, move the burgers to a cooler area of the grill (that is, the perimeter of the grate on a charcoal grill, or over a turned-off burner of a gas grill). Transfer to a platter. Add the rolls to the grill, cut sides down, and grill until toasted, about 1 minute. Add to the platter.

4. Place each burger on a roll and add 2 tomato slices and a lettuce leaf. Serve with the ketchup, Sriracha Aïoli, and mustard.

# Osso Buco

*contributed by* TONY COLABELLI

*Braised veal shanks give up a lot of gelatin during their long simmering, creating a sauce with an extra measure of richness. Serve it the classic way, with saffron risotto, or simply over pasta or rice—it's all good! The gremolata topping provides a counterpoint of bright, fresh flavor to the long-simmered, tender meat, so don't make the mistake of skipping it.* {MAKES 4 SERVINGS}

¼ cup plus 2 tablespoons extra-virgin olive oil

4 meaty veal shanks, about 1½ pounds each and 2½ inches thick

Kosher salt

Freshly ground black pepper

2 yellow onions, chopped

2 carrots, peeled and cut into ¼-inch dice

3 celery stalks, cut into ¼-inch dice

3 cloves garlic, crushed

2 tablespoons all-purpose flour

1 cup dry white wine, such as Pinot Grigio

1 can (28 ounces) plum tomatoes in juice, preferably San Marzano, chopped

2 cups reduced-sodium beef broth

1 teaspoon chopped fresh thyme

1 bay leaf

2 tablespoons cold unsalted butter, cut into tablespoons

GREMOLATA

¼ cup finely chopped fresh flat-leaf parsley

Grated zest of 1 lemon

1 clove garlic, minced

1. Heat the ¼ cup olive oil in a large Dutch oven or flameproof casserole over medium-high heat. Season the shanks with 2 teaspoons salt and 1 teaspoon pepper. Add to the Dutch oven and cook, turning occasionally, until browned on all sides, about 10 minutes. Transfer to a plate.

2. Add the remaining 2 tablespoons oil to the Dutch oven and heat. Add the onions, carrots, celery, and garlic and stir well. Cover and reduce the heat to medium. Cook until the vegetables soften, about 10 minutes. Sprinkle in the flour and stir well. Add the wine, stirring to scrape up the browned bits in the Dutch oven with a wooden spatula, and bring to a boil over high heat. Add the tomatoes with their juices, the broth, thyme, and bay leaf. Return the veal to the Dutch oven and arrange so the pieces are almost completely submerged in the cooking liquid, adding water if needed. Bring to a boil. Reduce the heat to medium-low. Cover and simmer until the veal is tender, about 2 hours.

3. Meanwhile, make the Gremolata. Mix the parsley, lemon zest, and garlic together in a small bowl. Cover tightly with plastic wrap and set aside at room temperature.

4. Using tongs and a metal spatula, transfer the veal shanks to a deep serving platter and tent with aluminum foil to keep warm. Boil the cooking liquid over high heat, stirring often, until reduced by about half, about 10 minutes. Discard the bay leaf. Remove the Dutch oven from the heat. Add the butter and stir until melted. Season with salt and pepper. Pour the sauce over the veal. Sprinkle with the gremolata and serve.

# Slow-Roasted Pork with Pickled Ginger Cherry Sauce

*↬ contributed by* MICHAEL NORTHERN

*Here, a tender and flavorful pork roast is combined with the assertive flavors of pickled ginger and dark cherries. This is a low-stress dish that is easy to prepare in advance, leaving you ample time to share with your friends and family.* {MAKES 6 TO 8 SERVINGS}

1 boneless pork shoulder blade roast, tied, about 3 pounds

3 cloves garlic, minced

Kosher salt

Freshly ground black pepper

PICKLED GINGER CHERRY SAUCE

1 tablespoon canola oil

6 cloves garlic, minced

2 large shallots, minced

⅓ cup balsamic vinegar

½ cup seasoned rice wine vinegar

¼ cup squeezed dry and minced pickled ginger, available at Asian markets

2 tablespoons pickled ginger liquid

1 cup cherry preserves

1 tablespoon plus 1 teaspoon Sriracha sauce

1. Position a rack in the center of the oven and preheat the oven to 325°F.

2. Rub the pork shoulder all over with one-third (3 cloves) of the minced garlic, 2 tablespoons salt, and 2 teaspoons pepper. Place in a roasting pan and roast, uncovered, until an instant-read thermometer inserted in the center of the pork reads 180°F, about 3 hours.

3. Meanwhile, make the Pickled Ginger Cherry Sauce. Heat the oil in a medium saucepan over medium-low heat. Add the remaining (6 cloves) garlic and cook, stirring often, until fragrant, about 1 minute. Stir in the shallots and cook until translucent, about 2 minutes. Add the balsamic and rice vinegars and increase the heat to medium-high. Bring to a boil and cook until reduced to about ¼ cup, about 10 minutes. Stir in the pickled ginger, pickled ginger liquid, and ½ cup water. Add the cherry preserves and Sriracha. Bring to a boil and cook, stirring often, until the sauce has thickened slightly, about 5 minutes. Remove from the heat and let cool.

4. After the pork has baked for 3 hours, spoon about ¼ cup of the sauce over the pork and continue roasting for 10 minutes. Repeat with another ¼ cup of the sauce and roast until the pork is glazed, about 10 minutes more.

5. Transfer the roast to a carving board and let stand for 10 minutes. Carve the pork and transfer to a serving platter. Serve warm, with the remaining cherry sauce passed on the side.

# Double-Cut Pork Chops with Char Siu Sauce

*contributed by* DANIEL WOOD

*Char siu (literally "fork roasted" in Cantonese) pork is coated with a sweet-and-salty sauce, hung by metal hooks, and cooked over a low flame. This delicious glaze works just as well with grilled pork chops.* {MAKES 4 SERVINGS}

**CHAR SIU SAUCE**

¼ **cup soy sauce**

¼ **cup hoisin sauce**

2 **tablespoons oyster sauce**

2 **tablespoons honey**

2 **tablespoons seasoned rice wine vinegar**

¼ **cup Chinese rice wine or dry sherry**

½ **teaspoon five-spice powder**

4 **double-cut pork rib chops, each about 14 ounces and 2 inches thick**

2 **teaspoons kosher salt**

1 **teaspoon freshly ground black pepper**

2 **green onions, sliced crosswise, including green parts**

1. To make the Char Siu Sauce, combine all of the ingredients in a heavy saucepan. Bring to a boil over medium heat, whisking often. Reduce the heat to medium-low and simmer, whisking often, to blend the flavors, about 5 minutes. Transfer to a bowl and let cool completely. (The sauce can be refrigerated in an airtight container for up to 2 weeks.)

2. Meanwhile, season the chops with the salt and pepper. Let stand at room temperature while preparing the grill.

3. Prepare an indirect medium fire in a charcoal or gas grill (see Note, page 18).

4. Brush the grill grate clean. Lightly oil the grill grate. Place the chops on the grill over the fire and close the lid. After 2 minutes, rotate the chops 90 degrees. Cover and grill 2 minutes more to create cross-hatch grill marks. Turn the chops and brush with some of the sauce. Cover, and grill for 2 minutes, then rotate 90 degrees, cover, and grill 2 minutes more. Turn the chops over and move to the cool area of the grate without the heat source. Brush with some of the sauce, cover, and continue grilling with indirect heat until the sauce is bubbling and the chops feel resilient when pressed in the center with a fingertip (protect your finger with a paper towel so you don't burn yourself on the hot glaze), about 10 minutes more for medium-well.

5. Brush the chops with one final thick coat of sauce. Transfer each chop to a dinner plate. Let stand for 3 minutes, sprinkle the green onions on top, and serve immediately.

# Greek-Marinated Pork Tenderloin with Tzatziki

*↬ contributed by* MARCUS MATUSKY

*A Greek buddy of mine taught me this dish of pork marinated in an aromatic mix of vinegar, lemon juice, oregano, and garlic, then grilled. Metal skewers work best for grilling, as wooden ones, even when soaked, can scorch from the high heat.* {MAKES 6 TO 8 SERVINGS}

MARINATED PORK TENDERLOIN

¼ cup red wine vinegar

¼ cup fresh lemon juice

¼ cup extra-virgin olive oil

1 clove garlic, minced

2 teaspoons minced fresh oregano

2 teaspoons kosher salt

½ teaspoon freshly ground black pepper

2 pork tenderloins (1¼ pounds each), silverskin trimmed, cut crosswise into ¾-inch-thick slices

TZATZIKI

½ seedless (English) cucumber, coarsely chopped

1½ cups plain Greek yogurt

1 tablespoon extra-virgin olive oil

2 teaspoons fresh lemon juice

1 teaspoon minced fresh dill

Kosher salt

Freshly ground black pepper

1. To prepare the pork, whisk the vinegar, lemon juice, olive oil, garlic, oregano, salt, and pepper together in a medium bowl. Pour into a 1-gallon lock-top plastic bag, add the pork, and close the bag. Refrigerate for at least 1 and up to 2 hours, no longer. Remove the pork from the marinade. Thread 4 or 5 pork slices onto 2 flat metal skewers held parallel to each other. (If the pork is on a single skewer, it will flop and be difficult to turn on the grill.) Let stand at room temperature for 30 minutes before grilling.

2. To make the Tzatziki, pulse the cucumber in a food processor fitted with the metal blade until finely chopped. Transfer to a colander. A handful at a time, wrap the chopped cucumber in a clean kitchen towel and wring to remove excess moisture. Put the cucumber in a medium bowl. Add the yogurt, olive oil, lemon juice, and dill, and stir to combine. Season with salt and pepper. Transfer to a serving bowl. Cover and refrigerate for at least 1 hour or up to 1 day to blend the flavors.

3. To make the Tomato and Artichoke Salad, combine the tomatoes, artichoke hearts, cheese, olives, onion, garlic, and herbs in a serving bowl, season with salt and pepper, and stir to combine. Cover and let stand at room temperature for at least 1 hour to blend the flavors.

4. Prepare a medium fire in a charcoal grill, or preheat a gas grill to medium (see Note, page 18).

## TOMATO AND ARTICHOKE SALAD

5 plum (Roma) tomatoes, seeded and cut into ¾-inch cubes

1 jar (6.5 ounces) marinated artichoke hearts, drained and coarsely chopped

½ cup (2½ ounces) crumbled feta cheese

½ cup pitted and coarsely chopped Kalamata olives

2 tablespoons minced red onion

1 clove garlic, minced

1 tablespoon minced fresh oregano

½ teaspoon minced fresh dill

Kosher salt

Freshly ground black pepper

Minced fresh oregano for garnish

Extra-virgin olive oil for drizzling

12 pocket pita breads, top 1 inch trimmed from each to form a pocket

5. Brush the grill grate clean. Lightly oil the grate. Put the pork on the grill and close the lid. Grill the pork until the undersides are seared with grill marks, about 1½ minutes. Rotate the pork 90 degrees, cover, and grill for 1½ minutes longer. Flip the pork and continue grilling, rotating the pork after 90 seconds, until the pork feels resilient when pressed with a fingertip, about 3 minutes more. Transfer to a platter. Sprinkle with the oregano and drizzle with olive oil. Let stand for 5 minutes.

6. While the pork is resting, add the pita breads to the grill, close the lid, and cook, turning once, until toasted and heated through, about 2 minutes. Transfer to a basket lined with a towel and wrap in the towel.

7. Serve the pork with the pita, tzatziki, and salad. Place a few slices of pork in a pita, add the tzatziki and salad, and eat.

# Pork Chile Verde

*contributed by* CLAIRE FANKHAUSER

*Chile verde, a pork stew laden with lots of green chiles, can be found in just about every restaurant in Santa Fe, but not in Seattle, so I have taken to making my own version. This is even better made a day ahead and reheated.* {MAKES 8 SERVINGS}

2 tablespoons extra-virgin olive oil, or as needed

2½ pounds boneless pork shoulder, cut into 1-inch cubes

1 large yellow onion, chopped

2 cloves garlic, finely chopped

2 jalapeño or serrano chiles, seeded and minced, or more to taste

1 teaspoon ground cumin

4 cups reduced-sodium chicken broth

1 bottle (12 ounces) dark beer

2 bay leaves

Kosher salt

Freshly ground black pepper

1½ pounds mild green chiles, such as Anaheim or poblano

4 tablespoons (½ stick) unsalted butter

¼ cup all-purpose flour

¼ cup chopped fresh cilantro, plus more for garnish

3 tablespoons fresh lime juice

Warm flour tortillas for serving

Lime wedges for serving

1. Heat the 2 tablespoons oil in a large Dutch oven or flameproof casserole over medium-high heat. In batches, add the pork and cook, turning occasionally, until browned, about 10 minutes. Using a slotted spoon, transfer to a plate, leaving the fat in the pot.

2. Add more oil to the pot, if needed. Reduce the heat to medium. Add the onion and cook, stirring occasionally, until translucent, about 5 minutes. Add the garlic, the 2 jalapeños, and the cumin and cook until the garlic is fragrant, about 1 minute. Return the pork to the pot. Add the broth, beer, and bay leaves and bring to a simmer. Season with salt and pepper. Reduce the heat to medium-low. Cover and cook, stirring occasionally, until the pork is almost tender, about 2 hours.

3. Meanwhile, position a broiler rack about 8 inches from the source of heat and preheat the broiler on high. Put the mild green chiles on the rack and broil, turning occasionally, until blackened and blistered on all sides, about 10 minutes. Transfer to a large bowl and cover tightly with plastic wrap. Let stand until the chiles are cool enough to handle, about 20 minutes. Remove the skin, seeds, and ribs from the chiles. Coarsely chop the chiles.

4. Stir the chiles into the stew. Simmer until the pork is fork-tender, about 20 minutes. Discard the bay leaves.

5. Melt the butter in a medium saucepan over medium-low heat. Whisk in the flour. Let bubble without browning for 1 minute. Whisk in about 2 cups of the cooking liquid. Stir into the pot and return to a simmer. Cook until the stew thickens and has no flour taste, about 10 minutes. Stir in the ¼ cup cilantro and the lime juice. Taste and adjust the seasoning with salt, pepper, and more jalapeño or serrano chiles, if desired. Spoon into bowls, garnish with cilantro, and serve hot, with the warm tortillas and lime wedges.

# Wisconsin-Style Bratwurst with Caraway Sauerkraut

⌒ *contributed by* RYAN DODGE

*There is nothing better than bratwurst for a proper tailgating menu. Growing up in Wisconsin, amid northern European food cultures, I learned how to really make bratwurst. The brats are grilled for smokiness, then simmered in dark beer and onions for deep flavor. My sauerkraut is prepared with wine and caraway seed to take it beyond the usual stadium stuff.* {MAKES 6 TO 8 SERVINGS}

### CARAWAY SAUERKRAUT

2 tablespoons unsalted butter

1 yellow onion, finely chopped

½ cup dry white wine

2 teaspoons caraway seeds

2 pounds refrigerated sauerkraut, rinsed and drained

### BRATWURSTS

2 bottles (12 ounces each) dark beer or stout

1 small onion, thinly sliced

2 cloves garlic, crushed and peeled

12 bratwursts

12 hot dog buns for serving

Horseradish mustard for serving

1. To make the Caraway Sauerkraut, melt the butter in a large saucepan over medium heat. Add the onion and cook, stirring occasionally, until translucent, about 5 minutes. Add the wine and caraway and bring to a boil. Stir in the sauerkraut. Reduce the heat to medium-low and simmer, stirring often, until the wine is almost evaporated, about 45 minutes. Keep warm. (The sauerkraut can be cooked, cooled, covered, and refrigerated up to 3 days ahead. Reheat before serving.)

2. Prepare a medium fire in a charcoal grill, or preheat a gas grill to medium (see Note, page 18).

3. For the Bratwursts, bring the beer and 3 cups of water just to a boil over high heat in a large saucepan. Add the onion and garlic. Set aside.

4. Brush the grill grate clean. Lightly oil the grill grate. Add the bratwursts and close the lid. Cook, turning as needed, until browned on all sides but not bursting, about 10 minutes. (It is important that the bratwursts cook at a moderate pace, because if they are cooked too quickly, they will burst and lose their juices.) Transfer to a disposable aluminum foil pan.

5. Place the foil pan with the bratwursts on the grill and pour in the beer mixture. Cover and cook, with the liquid at a bare simmer (or just under a simmer) for 45 minutes. For a charcoal grill, the fire will have burned down to low, so the mixture shouldn't boil. If the coals are too hot, use long tongs to spread them out in a thinner layer. For a gas grill, reduce the heat to low and adjust as needed.

6. To serve, transfer the bratwursts to a platter. For each serving, place a bratwurst in a bun. Use a slotted spoon to add the sauerkraut to the bun and serve hot, with the mustard.

# Sausage, Tomato, and Polenta Casserole

*contributed by* VICKI WILSON

*My family and I live in the Pacific Northwest, where sunset comes very early during the winter months. This leads to cocooning and preparing satisfying casseroles like this one, perfect for warming up the kitchen and your insides. If you don't have the time to make the polenta from scratch, use slices of prepared polenta.* {MAKES 6 SERVINGS}

### POLENTA

3 cups whole milk

1 tablespoon unsalted butter

1 teaspoon sugar

1 teaspoon fine sea salt

1 cup stone-ground yellow cornmeal

¼ cup freshly grated Parmigiano-Reggiano cheese

### SPICY PEPPERS AND ONIONS

3 tablespoons extra-virgin olive oil

3 cloves garlic, thinly sliced

½ teaspoon red pepper flakes

1 large yellow onion, cut into ¼-inch-thick half-moons

2 yellow bell peppers, seeded, deribbed, and cut into ¼-inch strips

1 pound sweet or hot Italian pork sausages, casings removed

1 can (15 ounces) tomato sauce

1 teaspoon dried oregano

½ cup (2 ounces) freshly grated Parmigiano-Reggiano cheese

8 ounces fresh mozzarella, cut into ¼-inch-thick half-rounds

8 to 10 fresh basil leaves, thinly sliced

1. Preheat the oven to 375°F. Lightly oil a 13-by-9-inch baking dish.

2. To make the Polenta, bring the milk, butter, sugar, and salt to a simmer in a heavy medium saucepan over medium heat, making sure the milk doesn't boil over. Gradually whisk in the cornmeal. Reduce the heat to medium-low. Simmer, whisking often, until the mixture is smooth and pulls away from the sides of the saucepan, about 10 minutes. Remove from the heat and whisk in the cheese. Spread evenly in the baking dish and set aside.

3. To make the Spicy Peppers and Onions, warm 2 tablespoons of olive oil in a very large skillet over low heat. Add the garlic slices and hot red pepper flakes and cook gently until the garlic is fragrant, about 1 minute. Add the onions and bell peppers, increase the heat to medium-high, and cook, stirring occasionally, until lightly browned yet crisp-tender, about 10 minutes. Set aside.

4. Meanwhile, heat the remaining 1 tablespoon oil in a medium skillet over medium-high heat. Add the sausage and cook, stirring often and breaking up the meat with the side of a spoon, until it loses its raw look, about 10 minutes. Stir in the tomato sauce and oregano.

5. Spread the sausage mixture over the polenta. Top with the spicy peppers and onions. Sprinkle with the Parmigiano and top with the mozzarella. Bake until bubbling, about 35 minutes.

6. Remove from the oven and let stand for 5 minutes. Sprinkle with the basil and serve hot.

# Peppercorn-Crusted Lamb Chops with Spicy Fig Jam

↜ *contributed by* TONY ZAMORA

*Tender lamb rib chops, cut from a roasted rack, are one of the most elegant entrées. A mix of four different kinds of peppercorns (also called a peppercorn mélange, and sold at specialty grocers and online) makes a colorful, as well as flavorful, crust. The fig jam sauce is simple and delicious.*

{MAKES 4 SERVINGS}

### SPICY FIG JAM SAUCE

1 cup fig jam, preferably Mission fig

4 teaspoons Sriracha chili sauce

2 tablespoons unsalted butter

2 tablespoons extra-virgin olive oil

2 racks of lamb, each with 8 ribs and weighing 1¾ pounds, fully trimmed and bones frenched (see Note)

4 teaspoons kosher salt

¼ cup coarsely ground peppercorn mélange (a mix of pink, white, black, and green peppercorns)

1. To make the Spicy Fig Jam Sauce, mix the jam, 2 tablespoons water, and Sriracha together in a small saucepan. Warm the sauce over low heat, stirring occasionally. Add the butter to the sauce and stir until incorporated. Set aside while cooking the chops.

2. Position a rack in the center of the oven and preheat the oven to 500°F. Brush 1 tablespoon of the oil over the lamb racks. Season with the salt. Spread the peppercorns on a cutting board. Press the top and sides of each rack into the peppercorns to coat. Set aside.

3. Heat the remaining 1 tablespoon oil in a very large skillet over medium-high heat. Add one lamb rack, top side down, and cook until browned, about 3 minutes. Transfer to a cutting board. Repeat with the second rack. Interlace the lamb racks, bones facing up, and return to the skillet. Roast until an instant-read thermometer inserted into the center of a rack and not touching bone registers 130°F, about 20 minutes, for medium-rare.

4. Let the racks stand at room temperature for 5 minutes. Cut between the bones into individual chops. Transfer 4 chops to each dinner plate and add a large spoonful of the sauce. Serve immediately.

↜ NOTE: *Frenching* is trimming the meat from an uncooked rib roast or rack to expose the ends of the rib bones. Frenched racks of lamb have become commonplace, especially with imported Australian or New Zealand lamb, and can be found at many supermarkets and price clubs. If you buy a rack of lamb with untrimmed bones, ask your butcher to remove the chine bone and french the rack for you.

# CHICKEN

# Sixth & Pine Seasoned Fried Chicken

*contributed by* MICHAEL NORTHERN

*Great fried chicken (and this is!) takes a little planning. For the best flavor, give the chicken its first coating the night before cooking to allow the flavorful seasonings to fully penetrate the meat. Of course, fried chicken is the ultimate picnic food, but it's also terrific for supper with Roasted Garlic Mashed Potatoes (page 191). The chipotle honey is optional, but it brings this dish firmly into the twenty-first century.* {MAKES 4 TO 5 SERVINGS}

### SEASONED FLOUR

2 cups all-purpose flour

¼ cup salt

2 tablespoons granulated garlic

1 tablespoon granulated onion

1 tablespoon dried oregano

1½ teaspoons dried basil

1½ teaspoons freshly ground black pepper

1½ teaspoons dried marjoram

1½ teaspoons dried thyme

1½ teaspoons rubbed dried sage

½ teaspoon cayenne pepper

1 chicken, about 3¾ pounds, cut into 8 pieces, breast pieces cut in half crosswise to make a total of 10 pieces

### CHIPOTLE HONEY DIP

½ cup honey

3 tablespoons minced canned chipotle chile in adobo

Canola oil for deep-frying

1. Start the chicken at least 4 hours or up to 24 hours before frying. To make the Seasoned Flour, whisk the flour, salt, granulated garlic, granulated onion, oregano, basil, pepper, marjoram, thyme, sage, and cayenne together in a medium bowl. Transfer half of the seasoned flour to a large paper bag. Cover and reserve the remaining seasoned flour at room temperature.

2. One piece at a time, add the chicken to the seasoned flour in the bag and shake to coat well. Transfer the chicken, without the pieces touching each other, to a rimmed baking sheet. Discard the flour in the bag. Cover the chicken with plastic wrap and refrigerate for at least 4 or up to 24 hours. The flour coating will become moist and sticky.

3. To make the Chipotle Honey Dip, mix the honey and chipotle in a small bowl. Let stand to blend the flavors while frying the chicken.

4. Add the reserved seasoned flour to a fresh paper bag. One at a time, shake the chicken pieces in the flour to coat again. Arrange the chicken on the baking sheet and let stand at room temperature for 15 minutes to set the coating.

5. Add 3 inches of canola oil to a large, heavy pot (preferably cast iron) and heat over high heat until the temperature reads 350°F on a deep-frying thermometer. Position a rack in the center of the oven and preheat the oven to 200°F. Line a rimmed baking sheet with a large paper bag.

*continued >*

6. Add the drumsticks and thighs to the hot oil and cook, adjusting the heat to maintain the oil temperature at 350°F, until lightly browned, about 6 minutes. Cover the pot and cook for 6 minutes. Uncover and continue cooking until the chicken is golden brown and an instant-read thermometer inserted in the thickest part of a piece of chicken reads 165°F, about 6 minutes more. Use a slotted spoon to transfer the chicken to the prepared baking sheet. Put the baking sheet in the oven to keep the chicken warm.

7. Reheat the oil to 350°F. Add the chicken breast pieces and wings to the oil and repeat, cooking at three 4-minute intervals (uncovered, covered, and uncovered) until the internal temperature is 165°F, about 12 minutes total. Transfer to the prepared baking sheet to drain. Transfer the chicken to a platter and serve warm.

# New Orleans Chicken and Andouille Étouffée

*contributed by* SEAN MILLER

*This simple one-pot dish is the ultimate New Orleans comfort food. Traditionally served with popcorn rice (which smells like but doesn't taste like popcorn), it makes a hearty meal sure to warm up everyone at the table.* {MAKES 8 SERVINGS}

2 tablespoons canola oil

8 ounces andouille or other firm, spicy smoked sausage, cut into ½-inch dice

1 pound boneless, skinless chicken breasts, cut into bite-sized pieces

Kosher salt

Freshly ground black pepper

3 tablespoons unsalted butter

1 large yellow onion, chopped

1 red bell pepper, seeded, deribbed, and cut into ½-inch dice

1 green bell pepper, seeded, deribbed, and cut into ½-inch dice

2 celery stalks, cut into ½-inch dice

8 cloves garlic, minced

⅓ cup plus 1 tablespoon all-purpose flour

1 teaspoon rubbed dried sage

½ teaspoon dried thyme

½ teaspoon dried oregano

½ teaspoon sweet paprika

¼ teaspoon cayenne pepper

4 cups reduced-sodium chicken broth

3 green onions, including green parts, thinly sliced

1. Heat 1 tablespoon of the oil in a heavy soup pot over medium heat. Add the sausage and cook, stirring occasionally, until lightly browned, about 5 minutes. Use a slotted spoon to transfer the sausage to a plate, leaving the fat in the pot.

2. Add the remaining 1 tablespoon of oil to the pot and heat. Season the chicken with 1 teaspoon salt and ½ teaspoon pepper. Increase the heat to medium-high. In batches, add the chicken to the pot and cook, stirring occasionally, until lightly browned, about 5 minutes. Using the slotted spoon, transfer the chicken to the plate with the sausage.

3. Reduce the heat to medium. Add the butter to the pot and melt. Stir in the onion, red and green bell peppers, and celery. Cover and cook, stirring occasionally, until the onion is translucent, about 6 minutes. Stir in the garlic and cook, uncovered, until fragrant, about 1 minute. Sprinkle in the flour and stir well. Add the sage, thyme, oregano, paprika, and cayenne and stir for 30 seconds. Cook, stirring, until the flour begins to brown, about 3 minutes. Gradually stir in the broth and bring to a boil, stirring often.

4. Meanwhile, start the Rice. Bring the rice, chicken broth, and salt to a simmer in a medium saucepan over high heat. Reduce the heat to low and tightly cover. Simmer until the rice is tender and has absorbed the broth, about 20 minutes. Remove from the heat and let stand until ready to serve.

*continued >*

**RICE**

**2 cups popcorn, basmati, or jasmine rice**

**4 cups reduced-sodium chicken broth**

**½ teaspoon kosher salt**

5. Return the chicken and sausage and any juices on the plate to the pot. Reduce the heat to medium-low and simmer until the chicken is opaque throughout, about 20 minutes. Season with salt and pepper.

6. To serve, put a large spoonful of rice in each deep soup bowl. Ladle in the étouffée and sprinkle generously with the green onions. Serve hot.

# Herb Roasted Chicken Breasts

*contributed by* VINCENT ROSSETTI

*I learned this recipe from my wife, who received it from two of our closest friends, Mary and Panos Panay. The simple use of fresh herbs and olive oil makes it a great go-to dish that can be prepared with little notice or advance preparation. I enjoy this dish with roasted vegetables, a big salad, and good company.* {MAKES 6 SERVINGS}

6 boneless, skinless chicken breast halves, 8 ounces each

½ cup chopped fresh basil

⅓ cup extra-virgin olive oil

2 tablespoons finely chopped fresh oregano

1 tablespoon finely chopped fresh thyme

3 cloves garlic, minced

2 teaspoons kosher salt

1 teaspoon freshly ground black pepper

Lemon wedges for serving

1. One at a time, pound a chicken breast between two pieces of plastic wrap with a flat meat pounder or rolling pin until the chicken is about ½ inch thick.

2. Whisk the basil, oil, oregano, thyme, garlic, salt, and pepper together in a large bowl. Add the chicken and toss to coat evenly with the mixture. Place in a 1-gallon lock-top plastic bag and seal. Refrigerate, turning the bag occasionally, for at least 1 or up to 3 hours.

3. Position a rack in the top third of the oven and preheat the oven to 400°F.

4. One at a time, remove the chicken breast halves from the marinade, letting the excess marinade drip back into the bag, and arrange the chicken in a roasting pan large enough to hold them in a single layer. Roast until the chicken is lightly browned and feels firm when pressed in the center with a finger, about 30 minutes. (An instant-read thermometer, inserted horizontally through the side of a chicken breast to reach the center, should read 165°F.) Transfer the chicken to a platter.

5. Tilt the roasting pan to pool the pan juices and skim off the clear yellow fat. Place the pan over two burners on high heat and cook until sizzling. Add 1 cup water and bring to a boil, scraping up the browned bits in the pan with a wooden spoon. Cook until reduced to ½ cup, about 3 minutes. Pour over the chicken. Serve immediately, with the lemon wedges.

# Grilled Mediterranean Chicken with Lemon-Herb Marinade

〰 *contributed by* JONATHAN ROHLAND

*When my family craves grilled chicken (a summertime favorite with backyard cooks from coast to coast), I soak the chicken in this Mediterranean-inspired marinade. The trick for grilled chicken is to keep it away from the heat source, as the dripping marinade and hot fat will cause flare-ups. For a more tailored dish, marinate and grill 6 on-the-bone chicken breast halves.* {MAKES 4 SERVINGS}

**LEMON-HERB MARINADE**

¾ cup fresh lemon juice

½ cup dry white wine, such as Pinot Grigio

½ cup extra-virgin olive oil

4 large cloves garlic, minced

3 tablespoons finely chopped fresh oregano

2 tablespoons finely chopped fresh rosemary

2 tablespoons kosher salt

2 teaspoons freshly ground black pepper

1 chicken, about 4½ pounds, cut into 8 serving pieces

2 lemons, halved crosswise

1. To make the Lemon-Herb Marinade, whisk the lemon juice, wine, oil, garlic, oregano, rosemary, salt, and pepper together in a large nonreactive bowl.

2. Place the chicken in a 1-gallon lock-top plastic bag and pour in the marinade. Squeeze all of the air out of the bag and seal it. Refrigerate for at least 6 or up to 24 hours, turning the bag occasionally to distribute the flavors evenly.

3. Prepare a hot indirect fire in a charcoal or gas grill (see Note, page 18). For both grills, put an empty aluminum foil pan on the empty (turned-off) area of the fuel bed and half-fill the pan with water.

4. Remove the chicken from the marinade and discard the marinade. Lightly oil the grill grate. Place the chicken, skin side down, on the cool side of the grill. Close the lid and grill, turning occasionally, until an instant-read thermometer inserted in the thickest part of a breast reads 165°F, or for about 45 minutes. During the last 3 minutes, lightly oil the lemon halves and place, cut side down, on the grill to char with sear marks.

5. Remove the chicken from the grill. Transfer the chicken breast halves to a carving board, and the lemon halves and remaining chicken pieces to a platter. Let cool for 5 minutes. Cut the chicken breast halves in half crosswise to make 4 pieces. Add to the chicken on the platter with any juices. Serve hot.

# Chicken Breasts Sautéed in Apple Cider

*contributed by* VICKI WILSON

*This sweet and savory dish comes together very quickly once the chicken is soaked in buttermilk (and a quick marinade of only an hour works fine, too). Reserve this for the cool autumn months, when apples are at their peak. The sauce does take some time to reduce, but when it does, the result is a rich "liquid gold."* {MAKES 6 SERVINGS}

6 boneless, skinless chicken breast halves, about 8 ounces each

1½ cups buttermilk

1 cup all-purpose flour

Kosher salt

Freshly ground black pepper

2 tablespoons extra-virgin olive oil, plus more as needed

2 tablespoons unsalted butter

2 Jonathan apples, peeled, cored, and cut into ⅛-inch-thick wedges

3 cups apple cider

2 cups reduced-sodium chicken broth

2 cups heavy cream

1 tablespoon chopped fresh chives

1. One at a time, pound a chicken breast half between 2 sheets of plastic wrap with a flat meat pounder or a rolling pin until the chicken is about ½ inch thick. Transfer the chicken to a large bowl. Add the buttermilk and toss to coat. Cover and refrigerate for at least 1 and up to 4 hours.

2. Position a rack in the center of the oven and preheat the oven to 200°F.

3. Mix the flour, ½ teaspoon salt, and ¼ teaspoon pepper in a shallow dish. One at a time, remove a chicken breast from the buttermilk and drain off the excess buttermilk. Coat with the flour mixture, shake off the excess, and place on a plate. Repeat with the remaining chicken. Let the chicken stand for 10 minutes to set the coating.

4. Heat the 2 tablespoons oil in a large skillet, preferably nonstick, over medium heat until the oil is shimmering. In batches, adding more oil as needed, add the chicken breasts and cook until the undersides are golden, about 5 minutes. Flip the chicken breasts and cook until the other sides are golden and the chicken feels firm when pressed in the center with a fingertip, about 5 minutes more. Adjust the heat so the chicken browns steadily but still has the full 10 minutes to cook through. Transfer the chicken to paper towels to drain briefly, then move to a baking sheet. Keep warm in the oven.

*continued >*

5. Melt the butter in the same skillet over medium-high heat. Add the apples and cook, stirring occasionally, until just tender, about 3 minutes. Transfer to a plate.

6. Add the cider, broth, and cream to the skillet and bring to a boil over high heat, making sure the mixture doesn't boil over. Boil, stirring often, until the mixture has reduced by about three-quarters and is the color of melted caramel, about 20 minutes. Return the apples and their juices to the sauce and simmer for 1 minute to reheat the apples. Season the sauce with salt and pepper.

7. Transfer the warm chicken to a platter and pour the sauce and apples on top. Sprinkle with the chives and serve hot.

# Chicken and Mushroom Piccata

*contributed by* JASON LONGFIELD

*Whenever I make this dish, the piquant flavors take me back to my grandmother's kitchen. Chicken piccata is a popular restaurant entrée that you can make at home. And that's a good thing, because it is also a dish that everyone loves. This version makes lots of luscious sauce, so be sure to serve it with steamed rice or pasta to soak up every last bit.* {MAKES 4 SERVINGS}

3 tablespoons extra-virgin olive oil

1 pound thinly sliced chicken cutlets

Kosher salt

Freshly ground black pepper

½ cup all-purpose flour

13 tablespoons (1½ sticks plus
   1 tablespoon) unsalted butter,
   cut into tablespoons

8 ounces cremini mushrooms, sliced

2 cloves garlic, minced

½ cup fresh lemon juice

½ cup dry white wine, such as
   Pinot Grigio

¼ cup reduced-sodium chicken broth

2 tablespoons rinsed and drained
   nonpareil capers

2 tablespoons finely sliced fresh basil

Grated zest of 1 lemon

1. Heat 2 tablespoons of the oil in a large skillet over medium-high heat. Season the chicken with 1 teaspoon salt and ½ teaspoon pepper. Dredge the chicken in the flour, coating both sides, and pat off the excess flour. In batches, add to the skillet and cook, turning occasionally, until golden brown and cooked through, about 4 minutes. Transfer to a plate and tent with aluminum foil to keep warm.

2. Add the remaining 1 tablespoon oil and 1 tablespoon of the butter to the skillet and melt the butter over medium-high heat. Add the mushrooms and cook, stirring occasionally, until they are lightly browned and sizzling, about 7 minutes. Stir in the garlic and cook until fragrant, about 1 minute.

3. Stir in the lemon juice, wine, and broth and bring to a boil over high heat, scraping up the browned bits in the pan with a wooden spoon. Boil until the mixture is reduced by half, about 5 minutes. Reduce the heat to very low. One tablespoon at a time, stir in the remaining 12 tablespoons butter, letting each addition melt before adding the next. Stir in the capers. Return the chicken and its juices to the skillet. Turn the chicken in the sauce until it is heated through, about 1 minute. Season the sauce with salt and pepper.

4. Transfer the chicken to a platter, spoon the mushrooms and piccata sauce evenly over the chicken, and sprinkle with the basil and lemon zest. Serve hot.

# Bánh Mì Vietnamese Spicy Chicken Sandwiches

*contributed by* PETER DUMALIANG

*The ingredient list for these sandwiches may look long, but the directions are quite easy. In fact, consider this a make-ahead meal, because time will allow the flavors to blossom. The components are used to build small flavor-packed sandwiches that will be as delicious in your home as they would be served straight from a street cart in Saigon.* {MAKES 12 SMALL SANDWICHES; SERVES 6}

## CITRUS MARINATED CHICKEN

½ cup fresh lemon juice

¼ cup fresh lime juice

¼ cup soy sauce

1 large onion, thinly sliced

3 cloves garlic, minced

¼ cup packed dark brown sugar

¼ cup granulated sugar

2 tablespoons kosher salt

1½ teaspoons freshly ground black pepper

12 boneless, skinless chicken thighs, 4 ounces each

## PICKLED VEGETABLES

½ cup seasoned rice wine vinegar

¼ cup distilled white vinegar

¾ cup granulated sugar

2 tablespoons kosher salt

¾ teaspoon freshly ground black pepper

3 carrots, peeled and cut into 3-by-⅛-inch matchsticks

8 ounces daikon (white radish), peeled and cut into 3-by-⅛-inch matchsticks

1. To prepare the Citrus Marinated Chicken, whisk the lemon and lime juices, soy sauce, onion, garlic, brown sugar, the ¼ cup granulated sugar, the salt, and pepper together in a nonreactive bowl, being sure to dissolve the sugars. Pour into a 1-gallon lock-top plastic bag. Add the chicken and close the bag. Refrigerate, occasionally turning the bag, for at least 6 or up to 24 hours.

2. To make the Pickled Vegetables, bring the rice vinegar, distilled vinegar, the ¾ cup granulated sugar, the salt, and pepper to a boil in a nonreactive medium saucepan over medium heat, whisking to dissolve the sugar. Reduce the heat to medium-low and simmer for 10 to 12 minutes. Pour into a nonreactive medium bowl and let cool completely.

3. Add the carrots and daikon to the vinegar mixture and stir. Cover and let stand for at least 1 or up to 6 hours. Drain, discarding the brine. (The vegetables can be stored in an airtight container and refrigerated for up to 5 days.)

4. To make the Sriracha Aïoli, whisk the mayonnaise, roasted garlic, chipotle adobo, Sriracha, and salt together in a medium bowl. (The aïoli can be covered and refrigerated for up to 5 days.)

*continued >*

SRIRACHA AÏOLI

½ cup mayonnaise

¼ cup mashed Simple Roasted Garlic
(page 34)

1½ teaspoons adobo sauce from canned
chipotle chiles in adobo

1½ teaspoons Sriracha chili sauce

½ teaspoon kosher salt

12 small oblong French rolls, split
lengthwise, lightly toasted in a broiler

1 English (seedless) cucumber, halved
and cut lengthwise into twelve
⅛-inch slices

36 fresh cilantro sprigs

1 long mild green chile, such as Fresno
or Anaheim, cut diagonally into
24 thin rings

5. Remove the chicken from the marinade. Heat a large nonstick skillet over medium heat. Working in batches, add the chicken and weight it down with a flat lid or heatproof plate smaller than the skillet. Cook, adjusting the heat as needed, until the underside is browned, about 6 minutes. Flip the chicken, replace the lid, and cook until the chicken shows no sign of pink when pierced in the thickest part with the tip of a small sharp knife, about 6 minutes more. Transfer the chicken to a carving board. Repeat with the remaining chicken. Let the chicken stand for 5 minutes before carving each thigh crosswise into 4 slices.

6. For each sandwich, spread about 1 tablespoon aïoli on a roll. Add a sliced thigh and top with a cucumber slice and a scattering of pickled vegetables. Add 3 sprigs of cilantro and 2 chile rings to each sandwich. Place 2 sandwiches on each plate and serve at once.

# Grilled Chicken Breasts with Red Chili Marinade

*↬ contributed by* SEAN MILLER

*This simple but flavor-packed chicken could be the hit of your next barbecue. Because it only needs an hour of marinating, it's perfect for entertaining on short notice, and you're likely to have all of the ingredients on hand. Serve it on a bed of salad greens, and you're good to go.* {MAKES 6 SERVINGS}

**RED CHILI MARINADE**

½ cup dry white wine, such as Pinot Grigio

¼ cup extra-virgin olive oil

3 tablespoons chili powder

1 tablespoon granulated garlic

1 tablespoon granulated onion

1 tablespoon kosher salt

1 teaspoon dried oregano, preferably Mexican

1 teaspoon freshly ground black pepper

6 boneless, skinless chicken breast halves (8 ounces each)

1. To make the Red Chili Marinade, whisk the wine, oil, chili powder, granulated garlic, granulated onion, salt, oregano, and pepper in a bowl.

2. Pound each chicken breast between two sheets of plastic wrap with a flat meat pounder or a rolling pin to an even thickness of ½ inch. Transfer to a 1-gallon lock-top plastic bag. Add the marinade and close the bag. Refrigerate, turning occasionally, for at least 30 minutes or up to 1 hour, no more.

3. Meanwhile, prepare a medium fire in a charcoal grill, or preheat a gas grill to medium (see Note, page 18).

4. Brush the grill grate clean. Lightly oil the grill grate. Remove the chicken from the marinade, letting the excess marinade drip back into the bag and leaving the seasonings clinging to the chicken. Place on the grill and close the grill lid. Grill, rotating the chicken 90 degrees after 2 minutes, until the underside is lightly browned, about 5 minutes. Flip the chicken, cover and continue grilling, rotating the chicken 90 degrees after 2 minutes, until the chicken feels firm when pressed in the center with a fingertip, about 5 minutes. Transfer to a platter, let stand for 5 minutes, and serve hot.

# Grilled Chicken Burgers

*contributed by* TONY COLABELLI

*If you have family members who don't eat red meat, you will be glad to have this recipe in your files. Chicken breast by itself is quite lean, so an olive oil mayonnaise (loaded with lots of "good" fat) provides moisture. Chopped vegetables and basil deliver extra flavor to save the burgers from blandness.* {MAKES 6 BURGERS}

**CHICKEN BURGERS**

½ cup mayonnaise, preferably olive oil mayonnaise

⅓ cup finely chopped celery

⅓ cup finely chopped yellow onion

3 tablespoons chopped fresh basil

2 teaspoons kosher salt

¼ teaspoon red pepper flakes

¼ teaspoon freshly ground black pepper

2¼ pounds ground chicken breast

1 cup panko (Japanese bread crumbs)

6 hamburger rolls, split

Dijon mustard, tomato ketchup, and mayonnaise for serving

Lettuce leaves, sliced tomatoes, and onion rings for serving

1. To prepare the Chicken Burgers, mix the mayonnaise, celery, onion, basil, salt, red pepper flakes, and black pepper together in a medium bowl. Add the chicken breast and panko and mix (your clean hands work best) until combined. Cover and refrigerate while preparing the grill.

2. Prepare a medium fire in a charcoal grill, or preheat a gas grill to medium (see Note, page 18).

3. Shape the ground chicken mixture into 6 equal patties. Press a 2-inch-wide crater in the center of each patty (this helps to keep the burger from shrinking during grilling).

4. Brush the grill grate clean. Lightly oil the grill grate. Place the patties on the grill and close the grill lid. Cook until the undersides are browned and seared with grill marks, about 5 minutes. Turn the burgers, cover, and cook until the burgers feel firm and spring back when pressed in the center with a fingertip, about 5 minutes. Transfer to a platter. Add the buns to the grill, split side down, and cook until heated through, about 1 minute. Add to the platter.

5. Place a burger in each bun. Serve hot, with the condiments, lettuce, tomatoes, and onion.

# SEAFOOD

# Roast Salmon with Tuscan Marinade

*contributed by* MICHAEL NORTHERN

*I created this herb-and-garlic-flavored mixture to be versatile and season a range of dishes, from salmon to chicken to vegetables and more. Note that the mixture is used more as an enveloping seasoning for food, and not as a "soak." It really shows its stuff on this simple seared and roasted salmon. Serve with the Herb-Roasted Marketplace Vegetables on page 178, if you wish.*

{MAKES 6 SERVINGS}

TUSCAN MARINADE

8 cloves garlic, crushed and peeled

¾ teaspoon kosher salt

½ cup extra-virgin olive oil

2 tablespoons coarsely chopped fresh
   rosemary

2 tablespoons coarsely chopped fresh
   flat-leaf parsley

1 tablespoon coarsely chopped fresh
   thyme

¾ teaspoon freshly ground black pepper

6 salmon fillets, preferably wild-caught,
   about 6 ounces each, skin and pin
   bones removed

1 teaspoon kosher salt

½ teaspoon freshly ground black pepper

2 lemons, cut into wedges

1. Position a rack in the upper third of the oven and preheat the oven to 400°F. Line a rimmed baking sheet with parchment paper.

2. To make the Tuscan Marinade, coarsely chop the garlic. Sprinkle with the salt and chop and smear the garlic on the cutting board to make a paste. Transfer to a blender. Add the oil, rosemary, parsley, thyme, and pepper. Process until the herbs are finely chopped, about 15 seconds.

3. Place the salmon in a large bowl. Add ⅓ cup of the marinade and spread on both sides with a rubber spatula. Season with salt and pepper on both sides. Preheat a large nonstick skillet over high heat. Place 3 fillets in the skillet, flesh side down, and cook until the edges begin to turn opaque and the flesh is deep brown in color, about 4 minutes. Transfer to the prepared baking sheet, flesh side up. Repeat with the remaining fillets.

4. Transfer to the oven and roast until the flesh is barely opaque when flaked with the tip of a knife, 10 to 12 minutes, depending on the thickness of the fillets. Use a spatula to transfer each salmon fillet to a dinner plate. Add the lemon wedges and serve hot.

**NOTE:** The recipe for Tuscan Marinade makes 1 cup, although you will need only ⅓ cup for this recipe. Refrigerate the extra marinade in an airtight container for up to 5 days, and use in one of the other recipes in this book.

# Baked Rigatoni with Spinach and Fresh Mozzarella

~ *contributed by* VINCENT ROSSETTI

*During the cold winter months, folks need a reason to get out of hibernation and socialize. I love to bake a big dish of this pasta and invite friends and family over to share and enjoy. And because it is made ahead of time, I get extra quality time with my loved ones. Open a bottle of red wine, break some crusty bread, and dish it up.* {MAKES 8 SERVINGS}

**GARLIC TOMATO SAUCE**

2 tablespoons extra-virgin olive oil

8 cloves garlic, thinly sliced
   (about ¼ cup)

2 cans (28 ounces each) plum tomatoes
   in tomato purée, preferably San
   Marzano

¼ cup coarsely chopped fresh basil

2 teaspoons kosher salt

1 teaspoon freshly ground black pepper

2 tablespoons extra-virgin olive oil

1 small yellow onion, chopped

2 cloves garlic, minced

1 pound spinach, stemmed, well rinsed
   but not dried, and coarsely chopped

1 pound rigatoni pasta

1 pound fresh mozzarella cheese, cut
   into ½-inch cubes

Kosher salt

Freshly ground black pepper

½ cup (2 ounces) freshly grated
   Parmigiano-Reggiano cheese, plus
   more for serving

1. To make the Garlic Tomato Sauce, warm the oil in a large saucepan over medium-low heat. Add the garlic and stir until it turns pale gold, about 1 minute. Add the tomatoes, including the purée, and simmer, stirring occasionally, until the sauce thickens and the flavors meld, 10 to 15 minutes. Using the back of a spoon or a potato masher, break the tomatoes into chunky pieces. Add the basil, salt, and pepper.

2. Preheat the oven to 350°F. Lightly oil a 9-by-13-inch baking dish.

3. Heat the oil in a large skillet over medium heat. Add the onion and cook, stirring occasionally, until softened, about 3 minutes. Stir in the garlic and cook until fragrant, about 1 minute. In batches, stir in the spinach, letting each batch wilt before adding the next. Remove from the heat.

4. Meanwhile, bring a large pot of lightly salted water to a boil over high heat. Add the pasta and cook according to the package directions until very al dente, about 2 minutes less than the cooking time recommended on the package.

5. Drain the pasta well and return to the pot. Add the tomato sauce, spinach mixture, and about three-quarters of the mozzarella and mix well. Season generously with salt and pepper. Spread in the baking dish. Top with the remaining mozzarella and sprinkle with the ½ cup Parmigiano.

6. Bake until the cheese is melting and the top is beginning to brown, about 25 minutes. Let stand for 5 minutes.

7. Spoon into warmed bowls and serve hot, with additional Parmigiano passed on the side.

# Gnocchi with Italian Sausage and Tomato Alfredo Sauce

꒰ *contributed by* MICHAEL NORTHERN

*Imported Italian gnocchi can be found in vacuum-packed trays right in the dried pasta section of most markets—just look for the Italian flag on the package. Using these gnocchi can produce some pretty remarkable results and certainly saves making a mess in the kitchen as well. Here, gnocchi are combined with a simple creamy tomato sauce and some zippy Italian sausage.*

{MAKES 6 TO 8 SERVINGS}

3 tablespoons extra-virgin olive oil

1 pound hot Italian sausage, casings removed

1 yellow onion, chopped

2 cloves garlic, minced

3 tablespoons all-purpose flour

3 cups heavy cream

1 can (6 ounces) tomato paste

Kosher salt

Freshly ground black pepper

3 pounds vacuum-packed imported gnocchi

4 ounces baby spinach

½ cup (2 ounces) freshly grated Parmigiano-Reggiano cheese, plus more for serving

1. Heat 1 tablespoon of the oil in a large, heavy saucepan over medium heat. Add the sausage and cook, breaking up the meat with the side of a spoon, until it loses its raw look, about 10 minutes. Increase the heat to high and cook, stirring occasionally, until the meat browns, about 2 minutes. Using a slotted spoon, transfer the sausage to paper towels to drain. Discard the fat and wipe out the saucepan.

2. Add the remaining 2 tablespoons olive oil to the saucepan and return to medium heat. Add the onion and garlic and cook, stirring occasionally, until the onion is golden and the garlic is fragrant, about 5 minutes. Sprinkle with the flour and stir well. Reduce the heat to low. Cook, stirring often without browning the flour, for 2 minutes. Stir in the cream and tomato paste and whisk well to dissolve the tomato paste. Increase the heat to medium-high and bring to a simmer. Cook, stirring often, until lightly thickened, about 3 minutes. Season with salt and pepper. Set the sauce aside.

3. Meanwhile, bring a large pot of lightly salted water to a boil over high heat. Add the gnocchi and cook according to the package directions until tender. Scoop out and reserve 1 cup of the pasta cooking water. Drain the gnocchi well. Return the gnocchi to their cooking pot.

4. Stir the spinach and sausage into the sauce. Add to the gnocchi, along with the ½ cup Parmigiano. Stir well. If the sauce seems too thick, stir in some of the reserved pasta cooking water. Taste and adjust the seasoning.

5. Divide the gnocchi evenly among warmed bowls. Serve hot, with additional Parmigiano cheese passed on the side.

# Homemade Fresh Egg Pasta

🌿 *contributed by* MICHAEL NORTHERN

*If you have ever wanted to make homemade pasta, this is the recipe for you. Compared to what you can find in a store, either dried or fresh, homemade pasta is worth the extra effort. It can be rolled out by hand, which takes a bit of effort and practice, or using a hand-cranked pasta machine, which is much simpler.* {MAKES ABOUT 1 POUND}

3¾ cups unbleached all-purpose flour, plus more for kneading

4 large eggs

2 teaspoons extra-virgin olive oil

Pinch of fine sea salt

1. Pour the 3¾ cups flour onto a work surface and shape it into a mound. Make a deep well in the flour and break the eggs into it. Drizzle the eggs with olive oil and sprinkle with the salt.

2. Using a fork, beat the eggs lightly for about 1 minute until they are blended; keep the flour mounded around the perimeter to ensure that no egg runs out. Gradually mix the flour into the eggs, a little at a time, until the mixture becomes too stiff to mix with the fork.

3. Knead the dough gently to incorporate as much of the flour as it will accept. You should now have a firm, smooth ball of dough and a scattering of loose dough bits that were not incorporated. To test the dough, wash and dry your hands, then press your thumb deep into the center of the mass; if it comes out clean, no more flour is needed. Put the dough to one side, and using a metal spatula or dough scraper, scrape the work surface completely clear of any flour or dough.

4. Sprinkle the cleaned work surface with more flour, place the dough on top, and knead the dough by pushing it down and away from you, stretching it out. Fold the dough in half, give it a half turn, and continue pushing it down and away from you. Keep repeating this action until the dough is smooth and firm, about 8 minutes. Wrap the dough in plastic wrap and let it rest for 30 minutes at room temperature to relax the dough and make it easier to roll out.

5. To roll out with a pasta machine, cut the dough into 4 pieces. Keep the dough you are not working with wrapped in plastic wrap. Run 1 piece of dough through the widest setting of the pasta machine 2 or 3 times, dusting the dough lightly with flour if it begins to stick. Fold the dough into thirds and set the machine to the next narrower setting on the dial, then run the dough through again. Repeat this folding step

**NOTE:** The rolling pin used for pasta is more like a dowel than a rolling pin with handles. It is typically 1½ inches in diameter and 32 inches in length and may be found at well-stocked kitchenware stores.

twice, lightly flouring the dough as necessary and adjusting the machine each time to a progressively narrower setting. You should now have a long, thin sheet of pasta. If the sheets become too long to work with easily, cut them in half. Continue running the dough through the machine, without folding the dough into thirds and using a progressively narrower setting each time, until the pasta is thin enough to see the shadow of your hand through when you hold it up to the light. Lay the finished sheets out on a lightly floured surface and let them dry for a few minutes before cutting them by hand or by the machine.

6. To roll the pasta out by hand, dust a large work surface with flour. Place 1 piece of dough on the surface and flatten it with the palm of your hand. Using a rolling pin (see Note), preferably a long, thin one, place the pin in the center of the dough and start rolling out toward the edge while stretching the dough with the pin at the same time. Pick the dough up, give it a quarter turn, clockwise. Keep rolling out toward the edge and turning the dough a quarter turn while rolling and simultaneously stretching out the dough. Dust the dough lightly with flour if it begins to stick. Work quickly, as the dough will refuse to give and may start to crack if it dries out. You should eventually have a large, thin smooth sheet of pasta that is thin enough to see the shadow of your hand through.

7. To cut using a pasta machine, attach the cutting rollers and run the sheets through the cutters. The wider rollers will cut fettuccine and the narrower ones tagliolini. To cut pasta by hand, loosely fold the sheets lengthwise, making a flat roll about 3 inches thick. Using a large knife, cut the roll about ⅓ inch wide for fettuccine, ¼ inch wide for tagliolini, or ¾ inch wide for pappardelle. Separate the strands and spread them out on a towel.

8. To cook the pasta, fill a large pot with about 6 quarts of water and bring to a rolling boil over high heat. Add 2 tablespoons of salt. Add the pasta all at once and briefly stir to prevent sticking. Very thin fresh pasta can cook in about 1 minute; thicker fresh pasta may take up to 3 minutes. Drain the pasta in a colander, toss with your favorite sauce, and serve immediately.

# Lemon-Scented Risotto with Seared Scallops and Green Beans

〜 *contributed by* TONY COLABELLI

*Risotto does require the cook to stir the rice for about twenty minutes—but aren't there days when standing in one place is a welcome change of pace? It can also be an opportunity for the family to gather in the kitchen and help with the various dinner chores. This is an elegant, upscale version.*

{MAKES 4 MAIN-COURSE OR 6 APPETIZER SERVINGS}

6 ounces haricots verts or small green beans, trimmed and cut in half

6 cups reduced-sodium chicken broth

4 tablespoons extra-virgin olive oil

½ yellow onion, chopped

2 cups Italian medium-grain rice, such as Carnaroli, Vialone Nano, or Arborio

½ cup dry white wine, such as Pinot Grigio

½ cup freshly grated Parmigiano-Reggiano cheese, plus more for serving

2 tablespoons unsalted butter

Kosher salt

Freshly ground black pepper

8 very large sea scallops, side muscle removed, patted dry

3 tablespoons fresh lemon juice

1. Bring a medium saucepan of salted water to a boil over high heat. Add the haricots verts and cook just until they turn a brighter green, about 1 minute. Drain, rinse under cold running water, and pat dry with paper towels.

2. Position a rack in the center of the oven and preheat the oven to 450°F. Bring the broth just to a simmer in a saucepan over medium heat. Reduce the heat to very low to keep the broth hot.

3. Heat 2 tablespoons of olive oil in a deep, wide saucepan or Dutch oven over medium heat. Add the onion and cook, stirring occasionally until translucent, about 3 minutes. Add the rice and stir until the kernels are covered with oil and the rice feels heavy in the spoon (do not toast the rice), about 2 minutes. Add the wine and cook, stirring occasionally, until the wine has almost evaporated.

4. Add ½ cup of the hot broth to the rice and cook, stirring frequently, until the rice has almost completely absorbed the liquid. Adjust the heat to medium-low to keep the risotto at a steady slow simmer. Continue adding the broth, ½ cup at a time, stirring until the broth is almost completely absorbed before adding the next addition and leaving ¼ cup for the final addition. After about 18 minutes, the rice grains should be creamy, plump, and cooked through but still slightly chewy. If you run out of broth before the risotto reaches this point, use hot water. Stir in the ½ cup Parmigiano cheese, along with the butter. Season with salt and pepper.

*continued >*

5. About 5 minutes before the risotto is done, heat the remaining 2 tablespoons oil in a large ovenproof skillet over medium-high heat until very hot but not smoking. Season the scallops with salt and pepper on both sides. Add the scallops, flat side down, to the skillet. Cook until the undersides are browned, about 1½ minutes. Turn and brown on the other side, about 1½ minutes longer. Scatter the green beans over and around the scallops. Place the skillet in the oven and cook until the scallops are barely opaque when pierced in the center with the tip of a small sharp knife and the green beans are heated through, 2 to 3 minutes. Season the scallops and green beans lightly with salt and pepper. Set the skillet aside.

6. Just before serving, stir the remaining ¼ cup broth and the lemon juice into the risotto. Season with salt and pepper. Divide the risotto evenly among warmed shallow bowls. Top each with equal amounts of the scallops and green beans. Serve hot, passing additional Parmigiano cheese at the table.

# Risotto with Corn and Roasted Mushrooms

*contributed by* ROB GIBBS

*Fresh corn in season is irresistible, and this recipe offers an alternative to the traditional corn on the cob so beloved at backyard barbecues. The corn cobs are simmered to make a broth that infuses the risotto with sweetness in every bite, balanced by the deep flavor of the mushrooms. This is a perfect vegetarian dish.* {MAKES 6 APPETIZER OR 4 MAIN-COURSE SERVINGS}

ROASTED MUSHROOMS

2 tablespoons extra-virgin olive oil

1 clove garlic, minced

1 pound assorted mushrooms, such as oyster, chanterelle, white button, and stemmed shiitake, halved lengthwise or cut into thick slices if large

Kosher salt

Freshly ground black pepper


3 ears corn, husked

5 tablespoons (½ stick plus 1 tablespoon) unsalted butter

1 small yellow onion, finely chopped

3 tablespoons finely chopped shallot

2 cups Italian medium-grain rice for risotto, such as Carnaroli, Vialone Nano, or Arborio

1½ cups dry white wine, such as Pinot Grigio

¾ cup (3 ounces) freshly grated Parmigiano-Reggiano cheese, plus more for serving

1. Position a rack in the top third of the oven and preheat the oven to 450°F. Lightly oil a rimmed baking sheet.

2. To make the Mushrooms, mix the oil and garlic in a large bowl. Add the mushrooms and toss well. Spread on the baking sheet. Bake, stirring occasionally, until browned on the edges, about 15 minutes. Season with salt and pepper. Set aside.

3. Cut the corn from each cob. Transfer the kernels to a medium bowl. Using the edge of the knife, scrape the corn "milk" from each cob and add the milk to the corn kernels. Repeat with the remaining corn. Cut the corn cobs into 2- to 3-inch-thick rounds.

4. Place the corn cob rounds in a large saucepan. Add 8 cups water and bring to boil over high heat. Reduce the heat to medium. Simmer briskly until reduced by one-quarter, about 15 minutes. Strain the corn stock through a fine-meshed sieve into a large bowl. You should have 6 cups. Return the stock to the saucepan and bring to a bare simmer over low heat.

5. Melt 1 tablespoon of the butter in a large skillet or Dutch oven over medium heat. Add the corn kernel mixture and cover. Cook, stirring often, until the corn is just tender, about 3 minutes. Transfer the corn to a bowl and set aside.

*continued >*

Kosher salt

Freshly ground black pepper

Chopped fresh chives for garnish

Aged balsamic vinegar or balsamic
reduction for serving (optional)

6. Melt 2 tablespoons of butter in a deep, wide saucepan or Dutch oven over medium heat. Add the onion and shallot and cook, stirring often, until the onion is translucent, about 3 minutes. Add the rice and stir until the rice feels heavy in the spoon (do not toast the rice), about 2 minutes. Add the wine and cook, stirring constantly, until the wine has almost evaporated.

7. Add ½ cup of the hot corn stock to the rice and cook, stirring frequently, until the rice has almost completely absorbed the liquid. Adjust the heat to medium-low to keep the risotto at a steady slow simmer. Continue adding the stock, ½ cup at a time, stirring until the broth is almost completely absorbed before adding the next addition and leaving ¼ cup for the final addition. After about 18 minutes, the rice grains should be creamy, plump, and cooked through but still lightly chewy. If you run out of broth before the rice reaches this point, use hot water. Remove from the heat and stir in the final addition of stock with the ¾ cup Parmigiano, half of the roasted mushrooms, and all of the corn. Stir in the remaining 2 tablespoons butter. Season with salt and pepper.

8. Divide the risotto evenly among warmed shallow bowls, topping with equal amounts of the remaining mushrooms. Sprinkle with the chives. Drizzle with the balsamic vinegar, if using. Serve immediately, with additional Parmigiano passed at the table.

# Asparagus Risotto with Chicken and Sun-Dried Tomatoes

*contributed by* MICHAEL NORTHERN

*Risotto, like pasta, provides a blank canvas for the cook's ingredients. Here, earthy asparagus, meaty chicken, and brightly flavored sun-dried tomatoes are combined to make a meal as appropriate for company as for a weeknight supper.*

{MAKES 6 APPETIZER OR 4 MAIN-COURSE SERVINGS}

6 cups reduced-sodium chicken broth

2 boneless, skinless chicken breast halves, about 6 ounces each

2 tablespoons extra-virgin olive oil

1 small yellow onion, finely chopped

3 tablespoons finely chopped shallots

2 cups Italian medium-grain rice for risotto, such as Carnaroli, Vialone Nano, or Arborio

½ cup dry white wine, such as Pinot Grigio

1 bunch asparagus, trimmed and cut into ½-inch rounds

3 tablespoons unsalted butter

¼ cup drained oil-packed sun-dried tomatoes, cut into ¼-inch dice

½ cup (2 ounces) freshly grated Parmigiano-Reggiano cheese, plus more for serving

Kosher salt

Freshly ground black pepper

1. Bring the broth just to a simmer over medium heat. Add the chicken to the broth, stir once, cover, and reduce the heat to low. Cover and simmer until the chicken shows no traces of pink when pierced at the thickest part with the tip of a sharp knife, about 12 minutes. Transfer the chicken to a plate and let cool, keeping the broth hot over very low heat. Cut the chicken into ½-inch pieces.

2. Heat the oil in a deep, wide saucepan or Dutch oven over medium heat. Add the onion and shallots and cook, stirring often, until the onion is translucent, about 3 minutes. Add the rice and stir until the rice feels heavy in the spoon (do not toast the rice), about 2 minutes. Add the wine and cook, stirring constantly, until the wine has almost evaporated.

3. Add ½ cup of the hot chicken broth to the rice and cook, stirring frequently, until the rice has almost completely absorbed the liquid. Adjust the heat to medium-low to keep the risotto at a steady simmer. Continue adding the broth, ½ cup at a time, stirring until the broth is almost completely absorbed before adding the next addition and leaving ¼ cup for the final addition. After cooking about 15 minutes, add the asparagus. Cook for 3 minutes, then stir in the butter, sun-dried tomatoes, and chicken. The rice grains should be creamy, plump, and cooked through but still lightly chewy. If you run out of broth before the rice reaches this point, use hot water. Remove from the heat and stir in the final addition of broth with the ½ cup Parmesan cheese. Season with salt and pepper.

4. Divide the risotto evenly among warmed shallow bowls. Serve hot, with additional Parmigiano passed at the table.

# SIDE DISHES & BREADS

# Herb-Roasted Marketplace Vegetables

*contributed by* MICHAEL NORTHERN

*Roasted vegetables are a deliciously colorful side dish, with the bonus option of cooking ahead and reheating. The key to success is to partially cook the "hard" vegetables before roasting. This is how we make them at our Marketplace Restaurants. Serve alongside Roast Salmon with Tuscan Marinade (page 136) for a delightful pairing.* {MAKES 6 SERVINGS}

3 unpeeled Yukon Gold potatoes, about 3 ounces each, scrubbed and halved lengthwise

¼ cup Tuscan Marinade (page 136)

Kosher salt

Freshly ground black pepper

2 ears corn, husked and cut crosswise into thirds

6 carrots of equal size, peeled

2 zucchini, cut crosswise on a sharp diagonal into thirds

1 large red bell pepper, seeded, deribbed, and cut lengthwise into 6 wedges

1 large yellow bell pepper, seeded, deribbed, and cut lengthwise into 6 wedges

1. Position a rack in the center of the oven and preheat the oven to 400°F. Bring a large pot of lightly salted water to a boil over high heat.

2. Toss the potatoes in a large bowl with the Tuscan Marinade. Season with salt and pepper and toss again. Transfer to a rimmed nonstick baking sheet, cut side down, letting the excess marinade drip back into the bowl. Bake until the potatoes are almost tender when pierced with the tip of a sharp knife, about 20 minutes.

3. Meanwhile, add the corn to the boiling water. Cook just until the corn turns a brighter shade of yellow, about 2 minutes. Using a wire-mesh skimmer or a slotted spoon, transfer the corn to a bowl of ice water. Add the carrots to the boiling water and cook until tender, about 3 minutes. Drain in a colander, rinse under cold water, and add the carrots to the ice water. Set aside.

4. When the potatoes are almost tender, drain the carrots and corn and pat dry with a clean kitchen towel. Add to the bowl with the marinade. Add the zucchini and red and yellow peppers and toss the vegetables to coat with the marinade. Season with salt and pepper and toss again. Remove the potatoes from the oven. Flip the potatoes over. Add the peppers, skin side down, and the corn around the potatoes. In another rimmed nonstick baking sheet, spread the remaining vegetables and their marinade in an even layer.

5. Return to the oven and continue baking until the bell peppers darken around the edges, the potatoes are tender and golden brown, and the carrots and zucchini are lightly browned, about 20 minutes. Serve hot.

# Grilled Summer Vegetables

~ *contributed by* ADAM WOHLER

*In the summertime, let Mother Nature help you in the kitchen by providing perfect seasonal vegetables to bring color and flavor to your table. Briefly marinated in our multipurpose Tuscan Marinade (page 136), summer vegetables emerge from the grill to be served as a light main course.*

{MAKES 6 TO 8 SERVINGS}

2 Japanese or white Thai eggplants, stemmed and cut lengthwise into ½-inch-thick slices

1 red bell pepper, seeded, deribbed, and cut lengthwise into quarters

1 yellow bell pepper, seeded, deribbed, and cut lengthwise into quarters

5 ripe plum (Roma) tomatoes, halved lengthwise

1 large zucchini, cut lengthwise into ¼-inch-thick slices

1 large yellow squash, cut lengthwise into ¼-inch-thick slices

12 green onions, including all but top 3 inches of green parts

½ cup Tuscan Marinade (page 136)

Kosher salt

Freshly ground black pepper

1 loaf crusty artisan bread, cut into ½-inch-thick slices

¼ cup extra-virgin olive oil for brushing

Balsamic vinegar for serving

1. Combine the eggplants, red and yellow bell peppers, tomatoes, zucchini, yellow squash, and green onions in a very large nonreactive bowl. Add the Tuscan Marinade and toss well. Season well with salt and pepper and toss again. Let stand while preparing the grill.

2. Prepare a medium fire in a charcoal grill, or preheat a gas grill to medium (see Note, page 18).

3. Brush the grill grate clean. In batches, if necessary, place the vegetables (bell peppers and tomatoes skin side down) on the grill and cover. Cook, arranging the vegetables on the platter as they are done: Eggplants: Cook, turning once, until lightly browned on both sides and tender, 8 to 10 minutes. Bell peppers: Cook, turning once, until the skins are blistered and blackened, 12 to 15 minutes. Tomatoes: Cook, turning once, until the tomatoes give off their juices, about 6 minutes. Zucchini and yellow squash: Cook, turning once, until the squash are seared with grill marks and crisp-tender, about 6 minutes. Green onions: Cook, turning occasionally, until lightly browned, about 4 minutes.

4. Brush the bread on both sides with the olive oil. Season with salt and pepper. Add to the grill, close the lid, and cook until lightly toasted, about 1 minute on each side. Transfer to another platter.

5. Serve the vegetables with the bread and balsamic vinegar, letting each person top the bread with vegetables and drizzle with the vinegar as desired.

# Cauliflower Gratin with Herbed Crumbs

*contributed by* JONATHAN ROHLAND

*As a child, cauliflower was never on my list of favorite foods. Now, I love eating it any way that I can: raw, roasted, or sautéed, or puréed with salt and pepper and olive oil. This warming recipe, with its rich sauce and crunchy topping, will make non-cauliflower eaters big fans of this versatile vegetable. It can be a vegetarian main course, or a side dish at a festive holiday gathering.* {MAKES 6 SERVINGS}

**BREAD CRUMBS**

½ cup panko (Japanese bread crumbs)

¼ cup freshly grated Parmigiano-Reggiano cheese

3 tablespoons extra-virgin olive oil

1 teaspoon minced fresh flat-leaf parsley

⅛ teaspoon dried thyme

Kosher salt

Freshly ground black pepper

1 head cauliflower, cored and broken into florets

3 tablespoons unsalted butter

¾ cup finely chopped yellow onion

¼ cup all-purpose flour

3 cups half-and-half

1 cup (4 ounces) shredded Jarlsberg cheese

Generous pinch of freshly grated nutmeg

Kosher salt

Freshly ground black pepper

1. Preheat the oven to 350°F. Lightly butter an 11½-by-8-inch baking dish.

2. To make the Bread Crumbs, mix the panko, Parmigiano, oil, parsley, and thyme in a small bowl until combined and moistened. Season with salt and pepper to taste.

3. Bring a large pot of lightly salted water to a boil over high heat. Add the cauliflower and cook until crisp-tender, about 5 minutes. Drain in a colander and rinse under cold running water. Drain well.

4. Melt the butter over medium-low heat in a large, heavy saucepan. Add the onion and cook, stirring occasionally, until translucent, about 2 minutes. Whisk in the flour and let bubble without browning for 1 minute. Whisk in the half-and-half and increase the heat to medium. Bring to a boil, whisking often. Remove from the heat. Whisk in ½ cup of the Jarlsberg cheese and the nutmeg. Season with salt and pepper. Add the cauliflower and stir well.

5. Spread the cauliflower and sauce in the prepared baking dish. Sprinkle with the remaining Jarlsberg, and then the herbed crumbs. Bake until the sauce is bubbling and the top is golden brown, about 30 minutes. Let cool for 5 minutes. Serve hot.

# Gratinéed Brussels Sprouts

*contributed by* SARELLE DROUGHT

*Try this great baked vegetable dish instead of ho-hum green bean casserole at your next holiday meal. Even the people who say they don't like Brussels sprouts will ask for seconds. The secret is a thick cloak of Gruyère cheese, which has a deliciously complex flavor with sweet, nutty, and salty notes. Oh, and a good dose of heavy cream doesn't hurt, either.* {MAKES 6 TO 8 SERVINGS}

4 tablespoons extra-virgin olive oil

4 ounces prosciutto, cut into ¼-inch dice

1¼ pounds Brussels sprouts, trimmed and halved lengthwise

¼ cup finely chopped shallots

⅓ cup dry white wine, such as Pinot Grigio

2 cups reduced-sodium chicken broth

½ teaspoon kosher salt

¼ teaspoon freshly ground black pepper

2 cups (8 ounces) shredded Gruyère cheese

2 cups heavy cream

1. Heat 2 tablespoons of the oil in a large skillet over medium-high heat. Add the prosciutto and cook, stirring occasionally, until browned, about 5 minutes. Use a slotted spoon to transfer the prosciutto to paper towels to drain.

2. Add the Brussels sprouts to the fat in the skillet and cook, stirring occasionally, until golden around the edges, about 10 minutes. Add the shallots and cook, stirring often, until they soften, about 2 minutes. Add the wine and cook until reduced by half, about 2 minutes. Add the broth and season with the salt and pepper. Bring to a boil. Cook, stirring occasionally, until the Brussels sprouts are tender and the liquid is reduced by half, about 20 minutes.

3. Preheat the oven to 375°F. Lightly butter a shallow 2-quart baking dish. Using a slotted spoon, remove the Brussels sprouts from the skillet and transfer to the baking dish, layering with half of the Gruyère. Boil the cooking liquid in the skillet until reduced to about 2 tablespoons, about 5 minutes. Add the cream, reduce the heat to medium, and cook the cream to reduce it by half, about 10 minutes more. Season the mixture with salt and pepper.

4. Pour the cream mixture over the Brussels sprouts. Scatter the reserved prosciutto on top, then sprinkle with the remaining Gruyère. Place the baking dish on a baking sheet. Bake until bubbling and golden brown, about 20 minutes. Serve hot.

# Glazed Carrots with Tarragon

*contributed by* MICHAEL NORTHERN

*Many people find it daunting to cook for a chef, but they shouldn't worry. We don't want to be dazzled—it's more important to share simple foods cooked with love. I learned this recipe, which is now a Northern family holiday essential, from my daughter, Vallary. Use fresh tarragon, as the dried will just not produce the same harmonious results.* {MAKES 4 TO 6 SERVINGS}

3 tablespoons unsalted butter

1½ pounds carrots, peeled and cut into
   3-by-¼-inch matchsticks

3 tablespoons packed light brown sugar

¼ teaspoon ground ginger

Kosher salt

Freshly ground black pepper

2 teaspoons minced fresh tarragon

1. Melt the butter in a large, deep skillet over medium heat. Add the carrots in an even layer, sprinkle with the brown sugar and ginger, and season with salt and pepper. Add ¾ cup water and bring to a simmer. Cover and cook until the carrots are beginning to soften, about 5 minutes.

2. Increase the heat to medium-high. Uncover the skillet and cook the carrots, stirring occasionally, until the water evaporates and the carrots are beginning to brown lightly around the edges, 5 to 7 minutes more.

3. Add the tarragon and toss to combine. Taste and adjust the seasoning. Serve hot.

# Sage and Parmesan Creamed Corn

〜 *contributed by* MICHAEL NORTHERN

*This recipe is at its absolute best in summer when fresh ears of corn are stacked high at your favorite market; as an added bonus the price typically falls to enticing levels at the same time. Always buy corn as soon as possible after it is picked, preferably from a market that buys locally grown corn. Peel back the husk and look for plump, full rows of kernels—if the kernels are flattened, the corn is likely old or overgrown and much of the sugar will have converted to starch. This dish is miles ahead of what you might remember about creamed corn in the past.* {MAKES 8 SERVINGS}

6 ears corn, husked

3 tablespoons unsalted butter

1 small yellow onion, finely chopped

3 cloves garlic, minced

3 tablespoons finely chopped shallots

¼ cup all-purpose flour

2 cups heavy cream

2 teaspoons minced fresh sage

½ cup freshly grated Parmigiano-Reggiano cheese, plus more for serving

Kosher salt

Freshly ground black pepper

1. Working with one ear of corn at a time, stand it upright, stem end down, on a cutting board. Use a sharp knife to cut downward along the cob, removing the kernels and rotating the cob a quarter turn after each cut. Scoop the kernels into a bowl. Using the edge of the knife, scrape the corn milk from the cob and add the milk to the corn kernels. Repeat with the remaining ears of corn.

2. In a large saucepan, melt the butter over medium heat. Add the onion, garlic, and shallots and cook, stirring occasionally, until the onion is translucent, about 5 minutes. Sprinkle in the flour and cook, stirring, for 1 minute; do not brown. Whisk in the cream and bring to a simmer. (The sauce will seem thick at this point.) Stir in the corn and the sage. Reduce the heat to medium-low and simmer, stirring occasionally, until the corn is tender, about 15 minutes. Remove from the heat and whisk in the ½ cup cheese. Season to taste with salt and pepper.

3. Transfer to a serving bowl, sprinkle with additional cheese, and serve hot.

# Creamy Parmesan and Fresh Herb Orzo

*contributed by* VINCENT ROSSETTI

*I love this recipe because it is simple but packs plenty of flavor. This is a great side with almost any roasted or grilled meat or seafood. I found it a great dish to use when I was introducing my children to the taste and flavors of fresh herbs. Creamy pasta with cheese is hard to beat!*

{MAKES 6 SERVINGS}

1 pound orzo pasta

1 tablespoon extra-virgin olive oil

1 small yellow onion, chopped

1 clove garlic, minced

½ cup (2 ounces) freshly grated
   Parmigiano-Reggiano, plus more
   for serving

1 tablespoon chopped fresh basil

1 tablespoon chopped fresh oregano

Kosher salt

Freshly ground black pepper

1. Bring a large pot of salted water to a boil over high heat. Add the orzo and cook according to the package directions until al dente.

2. Meanwhile, heat the oil in a large skillet over medium heat. Add the onion and cook, stirring occasionally, until translucent, about 5 minutes. Stir in the garlic and cook until fragrant, about 1 minute. Reduce the heat to very low.

3. Scoop out and reserve about 1 cup of the pasta cooking water. Drain the pasta well. Transfer to the skillet and stir well. Stir in the ½ cup Parmigiano cheese. Stir in just enough of the reserved pasta water (not necessarily all of it) to give the mixture a creamy consistency. Stir in the basil and oregano. Season with salt and pepper.

4. Spoon into warmed shallow bowls and serve hot, with additional Parmigiano passed on the side.

# Crisp Potatoes Anna

*contributed by* TONY ZAMORA

*A noble French potato dish, potatoes Anna is a golden, crispy cake with a creamy, tender interior. Extremely versatile, it can be served as a side dish to roast meat or chicken, but also try it for a casual brunch with eggs and sausage. You will need a mandoline or plastic V-slicer to quickly slice the potatoes into uniform rounds.* {MAKES 6 SERVINGS}

8 tablespoons unsalted butter

6 large baking (russet) potatoes, about
   2 pounds total

2½ teaspoons kosher salt

¾ teaspoon freshly ground black pepper

1. Position a rack in the center of the oven and preheat the oven to 350°F. Cut a 12-inch round of parchment paper to fit inside an oven-proof 12-inch-diameter (measured from the top) nonstick skillet.

2. Bring the butter to a full boil in a small saucepan over medium heat. Pour into a 1-cup glass measuring cup. Let stand for 5 minutes. Skim off the foam on the surface. Carefully pour the clear yellow clarified butter into a small bowl, leaving the milky residue in the cup.

3. Meanwhile, peel the potatoes. Immediately slice the potatoes with a mandoline or V-slicer into ⅛-inch-thick rounds. Do not rinse the potato slices.

4. Mix the salt and pepper together in a small bowl. Heat 4 table-spoons of the clarified butter in the skillet over medium heat. Starting at the center of the skillet, arrange the potato slices in an overlapping circular pattern at least 2 layers deep, occasionally seasoning the potatoes with the salt mixture. Cook until the potatoes at the edge of the skillet are beginning to brown, about 5 minutes.

5. Place the parchment paper round over the potatoes. Choose a flat lid or heatproof plate to fit inside the skillet. Brush the bottom of the lid with some of the remaining clarified butter and place the lid over the parchment-covered potatoes.

6. Bake until the potatoes are very tender when pierced with the tip of a sharp knife and are a rich golden brown around the edges of the skillet, about 45 minutes. Let cool in the skillet for 5 minutes. Remove the parchment and place a serving platter over the skillet. Carefully invert the potatoes and platter together to unmold the potatoes. Cut into 6 wedges and serve.

# Roasted Garlic Mashed Potatoes

🐟 *contributed by* MICHAEL THOMS

*Mashed potatoes are on the very short list of everyone's favorite comfort food. They are welcome at both special holiday meals and simple weeknight suppers. There are a few tricks to making perfect mashed potatoes (among them, draining the boiled baking potatoes very well before mashing, and using warm milk and butter), so follow this recipe carefully, and you will be very comforted.* {MAKES 6 TO 8 SERVINGS}

3 pounds baking (russet) potatoes, peeled and cut into 1½-inch chunks

4 tablespoons (½ stick) unsalted butter, cut into tablespoons

1 cup whole milk

2 tablespoons mashed Simple Roasted Garlic (page 34)

½ cup (2 ounces) freshly grated Parmigiano-Reggiano cheese

Kosher salt

Freshly ground black pepper

1. Put the potatoes in a large saucepan and add enough salted water to cover by 1 inch. (Taste the water—it should taste salty.) Cover the pot and bring to a boil over high heat. Reduce the heat to medium-low and uncover the saucepan. Cook, uncovered, until the potatoes can be easily pierced with the tip of a sharp knife, about 20 minutes.

2. Drain the potatoes in a colander. Cover with a clean kitchen towel. Let drain until the excess steam has been released and the exteriors of the potatoes look white and flaky, about 5 minutes.

3. Meanwhile, melt the butter in a small saucepan over medium heat. Add the milk and roasted garlic and stir just until warmed, about 1 minute. Remove from the heat.

4. Return the potatoes to their saucepan. Add the cheese. Whip the potatoes with an electric hand mixer set on medium speed, adding as much of the warm milk mixture as needed to give the potatoes the desired consistency of thick, thin, or somewhere in between. Season the potatoes with salt and pepper. Cover and let stand so the potato starch can absorb the liquid to make the potatoes easier to spoon onto plates, 3 to 5 minutes. Transfer to a warmed serving bowl and serve hot.

# Roasted Yukon Gold Potato Halves with Asparagus

↤ *contributed by* MICHAEL NORTHERN

*These multifaceted potatoes can be served with just about any grilled or roasted main course. Creamy Yukon Gold potatoes do not need to be peeled, so they can be readied for the oven in just a few minutes, and asparagus adds interest to this common side dish. Roasted potatoes are also a great salad ingredient—they are miles more interesting than boiled new potatoes—so I have included the recipe as a variation.* {MAKES 6 SERVINGS}

1½ pounds unpeeled Yukon Gold potatoes, about 4 ounces each, scrubbed and halved lengthwise

12 plump asparagus spears, trimmed, bottom 2 inches peeled with a vegetable peeler

3 tablespoons Tuscan Marinade (page 136)

½ teaspoon kosher salt

¼ teaspoon freshly ground black pepper

1. Position a rack in the upper third of the oven and preheat the oven to 400°F.

2. Toss the potatoes and asparagus with the Tuscan Marinade in a large bowl. Season with the salt and pepper and toss again. Arrange the potatoes, cut side down, on a nonstick rimmed baking sheet, letting the excess marinade drip back into the bowl. Set the asparagus and marinade aside.

3. Roast until the potatoes are almost tender when pierced with the tip of a sharp knife, about 30 minutes. Remove the baking sheet with the potatoes from the oven. Turn the potatoes over, cut side up. Remove the asparagus from the marinade letting the excess drip back into the bowl. Arrange the asparagus on the baking sheet, scattered between the potatoes. Roast until the asparagus is crisp-tender and the potatoes are golden brown and completely cooked, about 10 minutes. Serve immediately.

↤ **VARIATION** Roasted Yukon Gold Potatoes: Scrub 12 small unpeeled Yukon Gold potatoes (about 2 ounces each) and cut into quarters. Toss with 2 tablespoons Tuscan Marinade (page 136). Season with salt and pepper and toss again. Spread on a rimmed nonstick baking sheet. Roast in a preheated 400°F oven, turning the potatoes after 15 minutes. Continue roasting until tender and golden brown, about 20 minutes. Serve hot as a side dish, or let cool to room temperature to use as a salad ingredient.

# Maple Brown Butter Cornbread

*contributed by* PETER DUMALIANG

*Cooking butter to a light hazelnut brown intensifies its flavor. The trick is used here to give a new twist to cornbread sweetened with pure maple syrup. Serve it for supper with Sixth & Pine Seasoned Fried Chicken, page 117, or make it for breakfast as a great way to start the day.* {MAKES 8 SERVINGS}

1 cup fresh or frozen corn kernels

1 cup (2 sticks) unsalted butter, at room temperature

¾ cup medium-grain yellow cornmeal, preferably stone-ground

¾ cup all-purpose flour

1 teaspoon baking soda

½ teaspoon fine sea or table salt

¾ cup sugar

¼ cup maple syrup, preferably Grade B

4 large eggs, at room temperature

1. Position a rack in the center of the oven and preheat the oven to 325°F. Lightly butter an 11-by-7-inch baking pan.

2. Heat a heavy medium skillet, preferably cast iron, over medium-high heat. Add the corn and cook, stirring very occasionally, until lightly browned, about 5 minutes. Transfer to a plate and let cool.

3. Melt 6 tablespoons (¾ stick) of the butter in a small saucepan over medium heat. Cook until the milk solids in the bottom of the saucepan have turned hazelnut brown, about 2 minutes. Transfer to a bowl and let cool slightly.

4. Sift the cornmeal, flour, baking soda, and salt together into a medium bowl. Beat the remaining 10 tablespoons butter, the sugar, and maple syrup together in a medium bowl with an electric mixer on high speed until light and fluffy, about 3 minutes. Gradually beat in the eggs. With the machine on low speed, add the cornmeal mixture in three additions. Mix in the browned butter. Fold in the corn.

5. Spread the batter evenly in the prepared baking pan. Bake until golden brown and a wooden toothpick inserted in the center comes out clean, about 30 minutes. Let cool in the pan for 15 minutes. Cut into 8 pieces and serve warm.

# Honey and Thyme Dinner Rolls with Fleur de Sel

*↜ contributed by* JONATHAN ROHLAND

*One of the reasons why I am a chef is probably the aroma of my mom's freshly baked yeast rolls. I was driven to learn how I could make them, too. I have taken her recipe and made it my own using thyme, a finishing touch of a honey glaze, and a sprinkling of fleur de sel.* {MAKES 18 ROLLS}

**7 tablespoons (1 stick less 1 tablespoon) unsalted butter, cut up, plus 2 tablespoons, melted**

**½ cup whole milk**

**⅓ cup sugar**

**1 package active dry yeast (2¼ teaspoons)**

**1 large egg**

**4 cups unbleached all-purpose flour, as needed**

**1 tablespoon minced fresh thyme**

**2 tablespoons honey, warmed until fluid, for brushing**

**2 teaspoons fleur de sel Guérande or other fleur de sel, plus more for sprinkling**

1. Melt the 7 tablespoons butter in a small saucepan over low heat. Add the milk, ½ cup water, and the sugar and heat to 105° to 115°F. Pour into the bowl of a stand mixer. Sprinkle in the yeast and let stand until foamy, about 5 minutes. Whisk to dissolve the yeast. Whisk in the egg.

2. Fit the bowl on the mixer and attach the paddle beater. Add 1 cup of the flour, the thyme, and the 2 teaspoons fleur de sel. Mix on low speed, gradually adding the flour as needed to make a soft, tacky dough that pulls away from the sides of the bowl. Change the paddle for the dough hook. Mix on low speed (No. 2 on a KitchenAid mixer), adding more flour if needed, until the dough is smooth and supple, about 6 minutes.

3. Lightly butter a large bowl. Gather the dough into a ball and put in the bowl. Turn the dough to coat with butter. Cover with a damp kitchen towel or plastic wrap and let stand in a warm, draft-free place until doubled in volume, about 1½ hours.

4. Line a rimmed baking sheet with parchment paper. Punch down the dough. Divide the dough into 18 equal portions and shape each into a taut ball. Arrange the balls, seam side down and about 1 inch apart, on the prepared baking sheet and cover again with a damp towel. Let stand in a warm place until almost doubled in volume, about 45 minutes.

5. Meanwhile, position a rack in the center of the oven and preheat the oven to 375°F. Remove the towel. Brush the rolls with the 2 tablespoons melted butter. Bake the rolls until golden brown, 17 to 20 minutes. Remove from the oven. Brush the tops of the rolls with the honey and sprinkle with fleur de sel. Let cool slightly, then serve warm.

# Rosemary Biscuits

*contributed by* RICHARD SILVA

*These flaky biscuits are excellent on their own, or as an accompaniment for Chicken Pot Pie Soup on page 52. No matter how they are served, use a very light touch when making them, as overhandling leads to tough biscuits. In the case of biscuits, less is more.* {MAKES 6 BISCUITS}

2 tablespoons fresh rosemary leaves, minced

2 cups all-purpose flour, plus more for rolling out

1½ teaspoons baking powder

¾ teaspoon baking soda

1¼ teaspoons kosher salt

6 tablespoons (¾ stick) cold unsalted butter, cut into ½-inch cubes, plus 2 tablespoons, melted

¾ cup buttermilk

1. Position an oven rack in the center of the oven and preheat the oven to 400°F.

2. Bring a small saucepan of water to a boil over high heat. Add the rosemary and boil just until the rosemary turns a brighter green, about 1 minute. Drain in a sieve and rinse under cold running water. Drain again and pat completely dry with paper towels. (This helps the rosemary retain its color after baking.)

3. Sift the 2 cups flour, the baking powder, baking soda, and salt together into a medium bowl. Stir in the rosemary. Add the cubed 6 tablespoons butter and toss to coat. Use a pastry blender or two knives in a crisscross manner to cut in the butter until the mixture resembles coarse crumbs with some pea-sized pieces of butter. Gradually stir in the buttermilk until the mixture clumps together. Gather up into a ball. The dough should be moist and slightly sticky.

4. Turn the dough out onto a lightly floured work surface and knead once or twice to form a ball. Dust the top of the dough with flour and roll out about 1 inch thick. Using a 3-inch biscuit cutter, cut into 4 biscuits. Gather the dough scraps, gently form into a rectangle, and cut out 2 more biscuits. Transfer to a baking sheet, about 1 inch apart. Brush the tops with the 2 tablespoons melted butter.

5. Bake until the biscuits are well risen and golden brown, 16 to 18 minutes. Serve warm.

# Grilled Flatbreads with Herb Oil

~ *contributed by* ADAM WOHLER

*Get kids involved with making dinner, and you will instill in them an appreciation of good food for the rest of their lives. My daughter, Evelyn, loves to help make these herbed flatbreads. The yogurt adds an extra measure of flavor and helps tenderize the dough.* {MAKES 4 FLATBREADS}

FLATBREAD DOUGH

¼ cup warm (105° to 115° F) water

1 package active dry yeast
  (2¼ teaspoons)

1 tablespoon sugar

½ cup plain Greek yogurt

4½ cups unbleached all-purpose flour,
  as needed

2 teaspoons fine sea salt

HERB OIL

⅓ cup extra-virgin olive oil

1½ teaspoons chopped fresh rosemary

1½ teaspoons chopped fresh thyme

1½ teaspoons chopped fresh oregano

1½ teaspoons chopped fresh basil

2 cloves garlic, minced

1 teaspoon kosher salt

½ teaspoon freshly ground black pepper

1. To make the Flatbread Dough, put the warm water in the bowl of a stand mixer. Sprinkle in the yeast and let stand until foamy, about 5 minutes. Stir to dissolve the yeast. Add the sugar, yogurt, and 1½ cups cold water and stir to combine.

2. Fit the bowl on the mixer and attach the paddle beater. Add 1 cup of the flour and the salt. Mix on low speed, gradually adding the flour as needed to make a soft, tacky dough that pulls away from the sides of the bowl. Change the paddle to the dough hook. Mix on low speed (No. 2 on a KitchenAid mixer), adding more flour as needed to make a smooth, supple dough, about 6 minutes.

3. Lightly oil a large bowl. Gather the dough into a ball and put in the bowl. Turn the dough to coat with oil. Cover with a damp kitchen towel or plastic wrap and let stand in a warm, draft-free place until doubled in volume, about 1½ hours.

4. Meanwhile, make the Herb Oil. Combine all of the ingredients in a small bowl and let stand at room temperature for up to 1 hour.

5. Prepare a medium fire in a charcoal grill, or preheat a gas grill to medium (see Note, page 18)

6. Cut four 12-inch squares of parchment paper. Turn the dough out onto a lightly floured work surface and knead briefly. Cut the dough into 4 equal pieces. Shape each into a ball and cover with a kitchen towel. Working with one piece at a time, roll out the dough on an unfloured work surface into a 9-inch-diameter round about ¼ inch thick. Dust a parchment paper square with flour and transfer the dough round to the parchment paper.

7. Brush the grill grate clean. Lightly oil the grate. Carefully flip or slide one dough round off the parchment and onto the grill. Cook until the surface of the dough is bubbly, about 2 minutes. Brush the dough with herb oil, then turn the dough over and brush generously with the herb oil again. Cover and grill until the flatbread is cooked through and nicely browned, about 1 minute. Transfer to a rimmed baking sheet. Repeat with the remaining dough rounds, stacking them on the baking sheet.

8. Transfer the flatbreads to a cutting board, cut into serving portions, and serve warm.

# DESSERTS

# Pound Cake with Warm Berry Compote

*contributed by* JOAN HARNETT

*My great-aunt Genevieve's pound cake includes sour cream for added richness, flavor, and tenderness. Firm and buttery, it is wonderful with a big glass of cold milk for dunking. Also try it with the berry compote and perhaps a dollop of freshly whipped cream.*

{MAKES 10 TO 12 SERVINGS}

### POUND CAKE

3 cups all-purpose flour

½ teaspoon fine sea salt

¼ teaspoon baking soda

1 cup (2 sticks) unsalted butter, cut into tablespoons, at room temperature

3 cups sugar

6 large eggs, at room temperature

1 teaspoon pure vanilla extract

1 cup sour cream, at room temperature

### BERRY COMPOTE

2 teaspoons cornstarch

1½ cups fresh orange juice

3 tablespoons honey

1½ cups fresh blackberries

1½ cups fresh blueberries

3 cups fresh raspberries

½ teaspoon pure vanilla extract

1. Position a rack in the center of the oven and preheat the oven to 350°F. Lightly butter and flour a 12-cup Bundt pan, tapping out the excess flour.

2. To make the Pound Cake, sift the flour, salt, and baking soda together into a medium bowl. Beat the butter and sugar together in a large bowl with an electric mixer set on high speed until the mixture is light and fluffy, about 3 minutes. Gradually beat in the eggs, then the vanilla. Reduce the mixer to low speed. In thirds, alternating with two equal additions of the sour cream, beat in the flour until smooth, occasionally scraping down the sides of the bowl with a rubber spatula. Transfer to the pan and smooth the top.

3. Bake until the cake is golden brown and a wooden skewer inserted in the center comes out clean, about 1¼ hours. Transfer to a wire rack and let cool for 10 minutes. Run a dinner knife around the inside edge and tube of the pan. Invert the cake onto the rack and remove the pan. Let cool completely.

4. To make the Berry Compote, dissolve the cornstarch in ¼ cup of the orange juice in a small bowl. Bring the remaining 1¼ cups orange juice and the honey to a boil in a saucepan over medium heat, whisking often. Add the blackberries and blueberries and cook until they soften, about 2 minutes. Stir in the dissolved cornstarch mixture and bring to a boil, stirring constantly, for about 2 minutes. Remove from the heat and stir in the raspberries and vanilla. Transfer to a bowl and let cool slightly. Cut the cake into wedges and serve, topped with the warm compote.

# Red Velvet Cupcakes with Cream Cheese Frosting

*contributed by* TONY COLABELLI

*There is something alluring and elegant about red velvet, especially in the case of these little cakes. But don't expect a strong cocoa flavor, as it is used mainly to deepen the batter's hue.*

{MAKES 24 CUPCAKES}

### RED VELVET CUPCAKES

2½ cups cake flour (not self-rising)

⅓ cup Dutch-process cocoa powder

1½ teaspoons baking powder

1 teaspoon baking soda

⅛ teaspoon salt

1½ cups canola oil

2 large eggs, at room temperature

1½ cups granulated sugar

1 cup buttermilk

1 tablespoon red food coloring

1½ teaspoons pure vanilla extract

1 teaspoon cider vinegar

### CREAM CHEESE FROSTING

1 package (8 ounces) cream cheese, at room temperature

½ cup (1 stick) unsalted butter, at room temperature

1 teaspoon pure vanilla extract

1 teaspoon fresh lemon juice

2½ cups confectioners' sugar, sifted

24 fresh raspberries for garnish

Chocolate curls for garnish (see Note)

1. Position racks in the center and top third of the oven and preheat the oven to 350°F. Line 24 standard muffin cups with paper liners.

2. To make the Red Velvet Cupcakes, sift the flour, cocoa, baking powder, baking soda, and salt together into a large bowl. In another large bowl, beat the oil and eggs with an electric mixer on high speed until thickened, about 3 minutes. Gradually beat in the granulated sugar, then the buttermilk, food coloring, vanilla, and vinegar. In thirds, with the mixer on low speed, add the flour mixture, occasionally scraping down the sides of the bowl, and mix until smooth.

3. Divide the batter evenly among the muffin cups, filling each two-thirds full. Bake, with one pan on a rack, until a wooden toothpick inserted in the center of a cupcake comes out clean, about 20 minutes. Let cool in the pans for 5 minutes. Remove from the pans and transfer to wire racks to cool completely.

4. To make the Cream Cheese Frosting, beat the cream cheese, butter, vanilla, and lemon juice together in a large bowl with an electric mixer on high speed. With the mixer on low speed, gradually beat in enough of the confectioners' sugar to make a smooth, spreadable frosting. Frost the cupcakes with the frosting. Top each cupcake with a fresh raspberry and a few chocolate curls. (The cupcakes can be made up to 1 day ahead, stored in an airtight container at room temperature.)

**NOTE:** To make chocolate curls, let a chunk of chocolate (at least 6 ounces) stand in a warm place in the kitchen for about 1 hour. Working over a plate, use a vegetable peeler to shave curls from the chocolate. Refrigerate for at least 15 minutes to firm the curls before using.

# Pineapple Upside-Down Cupcakes

*contributed by* KERRI RUPELL

*As a lover of both pineapple upside-down cake and cupcakes, it seemed only logical to me to transform the old-fashioned cake into a miniature version. Although tailored for visual flair, this cupcake still serves up the traditional sweet flavors of a true pineapple upside-down cake.*

{MAKES 18 CUPCAKES}

### CARAMELIZED PINEAPPLE

1½ cups packed light brown sugar

8 tablespoons (1 stick) unsalted butter, cut up

Six ¼-inch-thick slices cored fresh pineapple, each cut into 6 equal pieces

### CUPCAKES

2 cups cake flour (not self-rising)

1¼ teaspoons baking powder

1 teaspoon baking soda

¼ teaspoon salt

1 cup buttermilk, at room temperature

2½ teaspoons pure vanilla extract

½ cup (1 stick) unsalted butter, at room temperature

1 cup granulated sugar

2 large eggs, at room temperature

18 Bing cherries, pitted and halved, or drained and halved maraschino cherries

1. Position racks in the center and top third of the oven and preheat the oven to 350°F. Line 18 standard muffin cups with paper liners.

2. To make the Caramelized Pineapple, cook the brown sugar and butter together in a medium skillet over medium heat, stirring often, until the mixture is melted and slightly thickened, about 3 minutes. Add the pineapple and cook, turning the pineapple pieces with tongs after 1 minute, until the pineapple looks translucent, about 2 minutes more. Using a dessert spoon, transfer 1 pineapple piece to each lined muffin cup, reserving the syrup.

3. To make the Cupcakes, sift the flour, baking powder, baking soda, and salt together into a large bowl. Mix the buttermilk and vanilla together in a glass measuring cup. Beat the butter and sugar in a large bowl with an electric mixer set on high speed until the mixture is light and fluffy, about 2 minutes. One at a time, beat in the eggs. With the mixer on low speed, add the flour mixture in thirds, alternating with two additions of the buttermilk mixture, occasionally scraping down the sides of the bowl, mixing until the batter is smooth.

4. Add a cherry half to each cup. Divide the batter evenly among the cups, filling each three-fourths full. Bake until a wooden toothpick inserted in the center of a cupcake comes out clean, about 20 minutes.

5. Let cool in the pan for 10 minutes. If the syrup is too thick to glaze the cupcakes, reheat the syrup and pineapple in the skillet. Top each cupcake with a pineapple piece and a cherry half. Spoon the warm syrup equally over the cupcakes. Let cool for 5 minutes. Remove from the pans, transfer to wire racks, and serve warm, or let cool completely. (The cupcakes can be made up to 1 day ahead and stored in an airtight container at room temperature.)

# Banana-Chocolate Cheesecake

*contributed by* RICHARD LADD

*I've been making this crazy-good cheesecake for family gatherings for as long as I can remember. Whenever I offer to bring something else, or try a variation, it is kindly suggested that I do not (repeat, not) rock the boat.* {MAKES 12 SERVINGS}

### GRAHAM CRACKER–PECAN CRUST

½ cup (1 stick) unsalted butter, melted

2 cups graham cracker crumbs (10 ounces)

½ cup very finely chopped pecans (use a food processor or blender)

### BANANA-CHOCOLATE FILLING

5 ounces bittersweet chocolate, finely chopped

2 pounds cream cheese, well softened at room temperature

2 cups sugar

5 large eggs, at room temperature

4 very ripe, soft bananas, peeled and mashed (about 2 cups)

1 tablespoon pure vanilla extract

1. To make the Graham Cracker–Pecan Crust, position a rack in the bottom third of the oven and preheat the oven to 375°F. Generously brush a 10-by-3-inch springform pan with some of the melted butter. Tightly wrap the outside of the pan with a double thickness of heavy-duty aluminum foil.

2. Mix the graham cracker crumbs, pecans, and remaining melted butter in a medium bowl until evenly moistened. Press firmly and evenly into the bottom and about ½ inch up the sides of the prepared pan. Place the pan on a baking sheet. Bake until the edges of the crust are beginning to brown and the crust smells toasted, 10 to 12 minutes. Transfer to a wire rack. Reduce the oven temperature to 300°F.

3. To make the Banana-Chocolate Filling, bring ¼ inch of water to a bare simmer in a skillet over low heat. Put the chocolate in a heatproof bowl. Put the bowl in the water, being sure not to splash water into the chocolate. Melt the chocolate, stirring occasionally. Remove the bowl from the water and let the chocolate cool until tepid.

4. Process the cream cheese and sugar in a food processor fitted with the metal blade until smooth, stopping the machine to occasionally scrape down the sides of the container. With the machine running, add the eggs, one at a time, again stopping to scrape down the sides of the container as needed. Add the mashed bananas and vanilla and process until combined. Scrape the filling into the crust. Drizzle the chocolate over the filling. Use a dinner knife or rubber spatula to swirl the chocolate into the filling, creating a marbleized pattern. Do not overmix.

5. Place the springform pan in a roasting pan large enough to hold it. Pour enough hot water into the roasting pan to come about ½ inch up the sides of the springform pan. Carefully put the roasting pan in the oven. Bake until the edges of the cheesecake are risen and very lightly browned, with a 1-inch-diameter area in the center that is unset, about 2 hours. Turn the oven off and let the cake stand in the oven with the door slightly ajar for 30 minutes.

6. Remove the springform pan from the water. Carefully remove and discard the foil. Transfer to the wire rack and let cool completely, at least 3 hours. Run a knife around the inside of the pan and remove the sides of the pan. Wrap the cheesecake in plastic wrap and refrigerate until chilled, at least 8 hours. (The cheesecake can be made up to 3 days ahead. It can also be frozen, wrapped in plastic wrap and an overwrap of aluminum foil, for up to 2 months. Thaw completely for 12 hours in the refrigerator.)

7. Let the cheesecake stand at room temperature for at least 1 hour. Use a thin, sharp knife, dipped into hot water between slices, to cut into wedges.

# Dark Chocolate Mint Cheesecake

*contributed by* MICHAEL NORTHERN

*While developing the line of Nordstrom Makers fine chocolates, we didn't tire of the taste of chocolate. In fact, we created this truly decadent symphony of chocolate and mint to celebrate the conclusion of the project. It will surely end up on your list of all-time favorite desserts.*

{MAKES 10 TO 12 SERVINGS}

### COOKIE CRUST

½ cup (1 stick) unsalted butter, melted

24 cream-filled chocolate sandwich cookies

½ teaspoon fine sea salt

### DARK CHOCOLATE MINT FILLING

10 ounces high-quality bittersweet or semisweet chocolate, coarsely chopped

1 cup heavy cream

½ teaspoon mint extract

½ cup unsweetened cocoa powder (not Dutch processed)

3 packages (8 ounces each) cream cheese, at room temperature

5 large eggs, lightly beaten

1½ cups packed light brown sugar

2 teaspoons pure vanilla extract

10 ounces Nordstrom Makers Dark Chocolate Mint candies, coarsely chopped

1. To make the Cookie Crust, preheat the oven to 375°F. Lightly brush the bottom and sides of a 10-by-3-inch springform pan with some of the melted butter. Line the bottom with parchment paper and lightly butter the paper.

2. Put the cookies in a 1-gallon lock-top plastic bag and, using a rolling pin, smash them to make coarse crumbs. Working in batches, transfer the cookie crumbs to a food processor and pulse until reduced to fine crumbs. You should have about 2½ cups.

3. Stir the cookie crumbs and salt together in a bowl. Stir in the remaining melted butter until the mixture is evenly moistened. Press the crumb mixture firmly and evenly into the bottom of the pan. Place the pan on a baking sheet. Bake until the crust is crisp and set, 10 to 12 minutes. Transfer to a wire rack. Reduce the oven temperature to 325°F.

4. To make the Dark Chocolate Mint Filling, bring 1 inch of water to a simmer over low heat in the bottom of a double boiler or saucepan. Put the chocolate, cream, mint extract, and cocoa in the top of the double boiler or in a heatproof bowl and place over (not touching) the water. Heat, stirring occasionally, until the chocolate melts and the mixture is smooth. Remove from the heat and let stand, stirring often, until the mixture is tepid.

*continued >*

5. In a food processor, process the cream cheese until lighter in texture. Add the eggs, brown sugar, and vanilla and process until thoroughly combined and smooth, stopping to scrape down the sides of the bowl as needed. With the machine running, gradually add the chocolate mixture in a thin, steady stream. Process until evenly colored, stopping to scrape down the sides of the bowl as needed. Using a rubber spatula, fold in the Nordstrom Makers Dark Chocolate Mint candies. Carefully pour the batter into the crust and smooth the top. Rap the pan against the counter to expel any trapped air.

6. Bake until the edges are puffed and have pulled away from the pan slightly and the center is barely set, about 1 hour. Turn off the oven and leave the oven door ajar. Let the cheesecake stand in the oven for 1 hour. Transfer to a wire rack and let cool completely. Cover with plastic wrap and refrigerate until well chilled, at least 6 hours or up to overnight.

7. To serve, run a knife around the inside of the pan to release the sides of the cheesecake, and then remove the sides of the pan. Slip a long, thin knife between the crust and parchment paper to separate them, and then carefully slide the paper out from under the cheese-cake. Use a thin, sharp knife, dipped into hot water between slices, to cut into wedges. Serve chilled.

# Berry Shortcakes with Lemon Curd and Blackberry Sauce

*contributed by* JASON LONGFIELD

*There are standard-issue shortcakes, and then there are those that stick in the memory. The contrast of the tart lemon curd with the sweet berries adds multiple layers of flavors that will have your guests swooning over just how good this dessert is. Use a gentle hand when mixing the dough, and try to serve the shortcakes when they are just cool enough to accept the billows of whipped cream without melting the topping.* {MAKES 8 SERVINGS}

### BLACKBERRY SAUCE

2 cups fresh or frozen blackberries

½ cup granulated sugar

3 tablespoons water

1 tablespoon fresh lemon juice

### SHORTCAKES

2⅔ cups all-purpose flour

⅓ cup plus 1 tablespoon granulated sugar

1¾ teaspoons baking powder

½ teaspoon baking soda

½ teaspoon salt

6 tablespoons (¾ stick) cold unsalted butter, cut into ½-inch cubes

¼ cup plus 3 tablespoons heavy cream

¼ cup plus 3 tablespoons buttermilk

1 large egg, beaten

2 tablespoons coarse raw or Demerara sugar

1. To make the Blackberry Sauce, bring the blackberries, the ½ cup sugar, 3 tablespoons water, and the lemon juice to a boil in a small nonreactive saucepan over medium heat, stirring to dissolve the sugar. Reduce the heat to medium-low and simmer, stirring occasionally, until the liquid has reduced by half, about 30 minutes. Transfer to a blender and, leaving the lid ajar to let the steam escape, purée. Using a rubber spatula, rub the sauce through a fine-meshed sieve into a bowl, discarding the seeds. Let cool. Transfer to a covered container and refrigerate until chilled, at least 3 hours. (The sauce can be refrigerated for up to 3 days.) If the sauce seems too thick, thin with water, stirred in 1 tablespoon at a time.

2. To make the Shortcakes, position a rack in the center of the oven and preheat the oven to 350°F. Line a rimmed baking sheet with parchment paper.

3. Sift the flour, the ⅓ cup plus 1 tablespoon sugar, the baking powder, baking soda, and salt into a medium bowl. Add the butter and toss to coat the cubes with the flour mixture. Using a pastry blender, cut in the butter until the mixture resembles coarse peas. Mix the cream, buttermilk, and egg together in a glass measuring cup with a fork until combined. Stir the cream mixture into the flour mixture to make a soft, shaggy dough. Do not overmix.

*continued >*

WHIPPED CREAM

1 cup heavy cream

¼ cup confectioners' sugar

¼ teaspoon pure vanilla extract

1½ cups Lemon Curd (page 217) or
 store-bought lemon curd

3 cups fresh raspberries

3 cups fresh blackberries

8 fresh mint sprigs for garnish

Confectioners' sugar for dusting

4. Turn out the dough onto a well-floured work surface. Sprinkle the top of the dough with flour. Pat the dough into a 4½-by-9-inch rectangle about ¾ inch thick. Cut the rectangle in half lengthwise, then crosswise into quarters to make eight 4¼-inch squares. One at a time, use your floured hands to pat and shape each square into a ¾-inch-thick round. Sprinkle the top of each shortcake with the raw sugar. Place on the prepared baking sheet, spacing the rounds about 2 inches apart.

5. Bake until risen and golden brown, about 20 minutes. Transfer to a wire rack and let cool for about 30 minutes.

6. To make the Whipped Cream, whip the cream, confectioners' sugar, and vanilla with an electric mixer set on high speed in a chilled medium bowl until soft peaks form. Cover and refrigerate until ready to serve. (The cream can be refrigerated for up to 1 day. If it separates, beat it until it thickens again.)

7. Split each shortcake in half horizontally. For each serving, place a small dollop of lemon curd in the center of the plate and set the shortcake bottom in the dollop. Top with about 3 tablespoons lemon curd and then a dollop of whipped cream. Add a large spoonful of each kind of berry to the shortcake, letting the berries cascade onto the plate. Finish with the shortcake top, placed off center on the bottom. Drizzle about 2 tablespoons of blackberry sauce on the plate around each shortcake. Add a mint sprig to the cream and dust with confectioners' sugar.

# Macadamia Nut Tart in Shortbread Crust

❧ *contributed by* MICHAEL NORTHERN

*Macadamia nuts are expensive, so you may want to reserve this recipe for special occasions. It must be served at room temperature and it can be made well ahead of time. I used to make the caramel in the filling and whipped cream topping from scratch until I discovered that store-bought works so well.* {MAKES 8 SERVINGS}

## SHORTBREAD DOUGH

1 cup (2 sticks) unsalted butter,
 at room temperature

¾ cup granulated sugar

1 teaspoon pure vanilla extract

1 large egg yolk

1½ cups cake flour (not self-rising)

½ cup cornstarch

¼ teaspoon fine sea salt

## MACADAMIA NUT FILLING

3 large eggs

1 cup store-bought caramel sauce

1 cup packed light brown sugar

1 teaspoon pure vanilla extract

¼ teaspoon fine sea salt

2½ cups unsalted macadamia nuts,
 toasted (see Note, page 216), cooled,
 and halved

1. To make the Shortbread Dough, beat the butter, granulated sugar, and vanilla together in a large bowl with an electric mixer on high speed, occasionally scraping down the sides of the bowl with a rubber spatula, until the mixture is light and fluffy, about 3 minutes. Beat in the egg yolk. Sift together the flour, cornstarch, and salt. Reduce the mixer speed to low and gradually add the flour mixture. The dough should be crumbly but hold together when pinched with your thumb and forefinger. Gather the dough together and shape into a thick disk. Wrap in plastic wrap and refrigerate for 30 to 60 minutes.

2. Roll out the dough between two 12-inch sheets of plastic wrap into an 11- to 12-inch round. Remove the top sheet of plastic. Invert and center the dough over a 10-inch round tart pan with a removable bottom, removing the plastic wrap. Fit the dough into the pan, being sure it fits snugly where the sides meet the bottom of the pan. Using your thumb, press the dough firmly into the pan, being sure that it reaches the top edge of the pan. Roll the rolling pin over the top of the pan to cut off and remove the excess dough. Freeze the dough-lined pan for 15 to 30 minutes.

3. Position a rack in the bottom third of the oven and preheat the oven to 400°F. Line the tart pan with aluminum foil and fill with pastry weights or dried beans. Place the pan on a baking sheet. Bake until the edges of the dough are beginning to brown, about 15 minutes. Remove the baking sheet and pan from the oven. Lift up and set the foil with the weights aside. Pierce the dough all over with a fork. Return the pan and baking sheet to the oven and continue baking until the pastry is golden brown, about 10 minutes. Transfer to a wire rack and let cool completely in the pan.

*continued >*

**CARAMEL WHIPPED CREAM**

1 cup heavy cream

¼ cup store-bought caramel sauce

1 tablespoon confectioners' sugar

½ teaspoon pure vanilla extract

¼ cup store-bought caramel sauce
   for serving

4. To make the Macadamia Nut Filling, whisk the eggs in a medium bowl. Add the caramel sauce, brown sugar, vanilla, and salt and whisk well to combine. Stir in the macadamia nuts. Pour into the tart pan, smoothing the top with a rubber spatula.

5. Reduce the oven temperature to 325°F. Bake until the filling is set (when you gently shake the pan, the filling will tremble as a unit, with the very center not quite set), about 45 minutes. Remove from the oven and let cool on the baking sheet for 10 minutes. Transfer the tart pan to a wire rack and let cool completely. Remove the sides of the pan. (The tart can be made up to 1 day ahead of serving, lightly covered and refrigerated. Remove from the refrigerator 1 hour before serving.)

6. To make the Caramel Whipped Cream, beat the cream, caramel sauce, confectioners' sugar, and vanilla together in a chilled medium bowl with an electric mixer set on high speed until soft peaks form. Cover and refrigerate until ready to serve, up to 3 hours.

7. Cut the tart into wedges. Serve with the caramel whipped cream and a drizzle of caramel sauce.

↬ **NOTE:** To toast macadamia nuts, spread them on a rimmed baking sheet and place them in a preheated 350°F oven. Toast the nuts, stirring occasionally, until they are fragrant and light tan in color, about 12 minutes. Pour onto a plate and let cool completely before chopping or halving.

# Lemon Curd Meringue Tart

*contributed by* MARCUS MATUSKY

*This wonderfully tangy tart is the creation of Beth Waldron, who cooked at our Seattle flagship café. Lemon meringue pie deserves its proud reputation, but the traditional filling pales next to this buttery and pleasantly puckery curd. Add a cookie-like crust and airy meringue, and you have a fine dessert to make during the winter citrus season when most local fruits are on hiatus.*

{MAKES 8 SERVINGS}

### TART DOUGH

4 tablespoons (½ stick) unsalted butter, at room temperature

½ cup sugar

¼ teaspoon kosher salt

1 large egg yolk (save the white for the meringue)

1 cup cake flour (not self-rising)

### LEMON CURD

1½ cups sugar

4 large eggs

¾ cup fresh lemon juice

12 tablespoons (1½ sticks) cold unsalted butter, cut into tablespoons

Grated zest of 1 lemon

### MERINGUE

3 large egg whites

⅓ cup plus 1 tablespoon sugar

1. To make the Tart Dough, beat the butter, sugar, and salt together in a medium bowl with an electric mixer on high speed until the mixture is light and fluffy, about 3 minutes. Beat in the egg yolk. Stir in the flour to make a soft dough. Gather up the dough, wrap in plastic wrap, and form into a thick disk. Refrigerate until chilled and firm enough to roll out, about 2 hours. (The dough can be made up to 2 days ahead. Let stand at room temperature for 10 minutes and rap firmly with a rolling pin to soften slightly before rolling out.)

2. Roll out the dough on a lightly floured work surface into a ⅛-inch-thick round. Transfer to a 9-inch tart pan with a removable bottom, being sure that the dough fits snugly where the bottom meets the sides. Let the excess dough hang over the sides. Run the rolling pin over the top of the pan to remove the excess dough. Press the dough firmly into the sides of the pan, letting the dough rise slightly over the edge of the pan. Pierce the dough all over with the tines of a fork. Put in the freezer for 15 minutes while preheating the oven.

3. Position a rack in the bottom third of the oven and preheat the oven to 400°F. Line the tart pan with aluminum foil and fill with pastry weights or dried beans. Place the pan on a baking sheet. Bake until the edges of the dough are beginning to brown, about 15 minutes. Remove the tart pan and baking sheet from the oven. Lift up and set the foil with the weights aside. Pierce the dough all over with a fork. Return the tart pan and baking sheet to the oven and continue baking until the pastry is golden brown, about 10 minutes. Transfer to a wire rack and let cool completely in the pan.

*continued >*

4. To make the Lemon Curd, place a fine-meshed sieve over a heat-proof medium bowl near the stove. Whisk the sugar and eggs together in a medium bowl until pale yellow and thickened, about 1 minute. Whisk in the lemon juice. Transfer to a heavy medium saucepan. Add the butter. Cook over medium-low heat, stirring constantly with a heatproof spatula and scraping down the sides of the pan, until the butter has melted and the mixture is thick enough to coat the spatula (an instant-read thermometer will read 185°F), about 5 minutes. Strain through the sieve to assure a smooth texture. Add the lemon zest to the curd and stir well. Spread evenly in the cooled tart shell.

5. Position a broiler rack about 8 inches from the source of heat and preheat the broiler.

6. Whip the egg whites in a medium bowl with an electric mixer on high speed until soft peaks form. One tablespoon at a time, beat in the sugar to form stiff, shiny peaks. Spread the meringue with a metal spatula or spoon over the hot filling, swirling the meringue into peaks. Broil, watching carefully, until the meringue is lightly browned, about 1 minute. Return to the wire rack and let cool completely. Remove the sides of the pan, slice, and serve.

# Dark Chocolate–Sea Salt Caramel Cookies

*↜ contributed by* DANIEL WOOD

*In this updated version of chocolate chip cookies, a split chocolate-covered caramel is perched on top of each cookie to make a gooey treat. If you use candies that do not have sea salt, add a sprinkle of flaky sea salt, such as fleur de sel de Guérande or Maldon, on the cookies as soon as they come out of the oven.* {MAKES 24 COOKIES}

1⅔ cups all-purpose flour

1 teaspoon baking powder

½ teaspoon baking soda

½ teaspoon fine sea salt

½ cup plus 2 tablespoons (1¼ sticks) unsalted butter, at room temperature

1⅓ cups packed light brown sugar

1⅓ cups granulated sugar

2 large eggs

2 teaspoons pure vanilla extract

24 Nordstrom Makers Dark Chocolate Sea Salt Caramels, halved lengthwise

1. Position racks in the top third and center of the oven and preheat the oven to 375°F. Line 3 rimmed baking sheets with parchment paper.

2. Sift the flour, baking powder, baking soda, and salt together in a medium bowl. Beat the butter in a large bowl with an electric mixer on high speed until smooth and creamy, about 1 minute. Gradually beat in the brown and granulated sugars and mix just until combined. Do not overmix. Gradually beat in the eggs, then the vanilla. With the mixer on low speed, mix in the flour in two additions.

3. Using a 1-ounce-portion scoop (about 2 tablespoons) for each, roll the dough into 24 balls between your palms. Arrange 8 balls on each baking sheet, spacing them well apart. Using the flat bottom of a drinking glass or a metal spatula, flatten each ball to a 1½-inch-diameter disk. It may be necessary to clean the glass or spatula occasionally to keep it from sticking to the cookie dough.

4. Bake two pans at a time until the cookies are set and the edges are barely beginning to color, about 8 minutes. Remove the pans from the oven. Quickly place and gently press 2 caramel halves, cut sides down, into the center of each cookie. Return the pans to the oven, switching their positions from top to bottom and front to back, and bake until the cookies are lightly browned, about 3 minutes more. Let cool on the pans for 5 minutes. Transfer to wire racks and let cool completely. Repeat, baking the third baking sheet of cookies on the center rack. (The cookies can be stored, separated by sheets of parchment or waxed paper, in airtight containers for up to 5 days.)

# The Ultimate Sugar Cookie

↩ *contributed by* DANIEL WOOD

*Get ready to fill your cookie jar with these old-fashioned treats. Chewy and tender at the same time, they live up to their hyperbolic name. Other recipes lack the cream cheese and buttermilk that give these cookies a melt-in-your mouth quality.* {MAKES 24 COOKIES}

2½ cups unbleached all-purpose flour

1 teaspoon baking powder

½ teaspoon baking soda

½ teaspoon fine sea salt

1½ cups sugar, plus ¼ cup more for coating and sprinkling

2 ounces cream cheese, cut into 1-inch chunks, at room temperature

6 tablespoons unsalted butter, melted and warm

⅓ cup canola oil

1 large egg

1 tablespoon buttermilk

2 teaspoons pure vanilla extract

1. Position racks in the upper third and center of the oven and preheat the oven to 350°F. Line 2 rimmed baking sheets with parchment paper.

2. Sift the flour, baking powder, baking soda, and salt together into a medium bowl. Whisk 1½ cups of the sugar, the cream cheese, and the warm melted butter together in a large bowl until the cheese softens and the mixture is smooth. Add the oil, egg, buttermilk, and vanilla and whisk again. Gradually stir in the flour mixture to make a soft dough.

3. Using about 2 tablespoons for each one, roll the dough into twenty-four 1½-inch-diameter balls. A few at a time, roll the balls in the sugar to coat. Place about 1½ inches apart on the prepared baking sheets. Use the flat bottom of a drinking glass or a wide metal spatula to press each ball into a 2-inch-diameter disk. Sprinkle the tops with the remaining sugar.

4. Bake for 6 minutes. Rotate the baking sheets from the top to bottom and front to back, and continue baking just until the cookies are beginning to brown around the edges, about 6 minutes.

5. Let cool on the baking sheets for 5 minutes. Transfer the cookies to wire racks and let cool completely. (The cookies can be stored in airtight containers for up to 5 days.)

# Butterscotch Pots de Crème with Fleur de Sel

*~ contributed by* RICHARD SILVA

*Pots de crème, members of the custard family, have a high cream content that gives them an even silkier texture than crème brûlée. A few flakes of fleur de sel accent the slight bitterness of the butterscotch.* {MAKES 6 SERVINGS}

**2 cups heavy cream**

**1 cup whole milk**

**¼ cup packed dark brown sugar**

**¾ cup granulated sugar**

**6 large egg yolks**

**1 teaspoon pure vanilla extract**

**¼ teaspoon fleur de sel de Guérande or other fleur de sel, plus more for garnish**

1. Preheat the oven to 300°F.

2. Bring the cream, milk, and brown sugar to a bare simmer in a saucepan over medium heat, stirring often to dissolve the sugar. Do not boil. Remove from the heat.

3. Stir the granulated sugar and ¼ cup water in a large saucepan over high heat until the sugar dissolves. Cook, swirling the saucepan by the handle and washing down the sugar crystals that form inside the pan with a natural-bristle brush dipped in cold water, until the mixture is smoking and the color of an old copper penny, about 4 minutes. Reduce the heat to very low. Gradually whisk in the hot cream mixture (the caramel will splatter) and cook over low heat until the caramel is completely dissolved. Remove from the heat.

4. Whisk the yolks in a heatproof medium bowl. Gradually whisk in the hot cream mixture. Whisk in the vanilla and ¼ teaspoon fleur de sel. Strain through a fine-meshed sieve into a 1-quart measuring cup or pitcher. Divide the custard among six 6-ounce pot de crème pots, custard cups, or ramekins.

5. Place the cups in a roasting pan. Carefully pour ½ inch of hot water into the roasting pan. Gently put the roasting pan in the oven. Bake until the custards are set (when you gently shake a cup, the custard will tremble as a unit, with the very center not quite set), 35 to 40 minutes. Remove the roasting pan from the oven and the cups from the pan. Let cool completely.

6. Cover each custard with plastic wrap. Refrigerate until chilled, at least 2 hours or up to overnight. Before serving, top each pot de crème with a pinch of fleur de sel. Serve chilled.

# Hot Fudge Sundaes in Warm Cookie Bowls

↜ *contributed by* MICHAEL NORTHERN

*Warm-from-the-oven cookies can be molded in a bowl shape to hold your favorite ice cream. I use prepared cookie dough here to keep things simple, but make your family's favorite chocolate chip cookie recipe if you have the time. At my house, this is a surefire favorite.* {MAKES 8 SERVINGS}

HOT FUDGE SAUCE

½ cup (1 stick) unsalted butter

½ cup light corn syrup

⅓ cup sugar

¼ cup Dutch-processed cocoa powder

4 ounces bittersweet chocolate, coarsely chopped

1 teaspoon pure vanilla extract

Pinch of fine sea salt

2 packages (1 pound each) prepared chocolate chip cookie dough

½ gallon vanilla ice cream

Whipped cream (optional)

1. Position oven racks in the top third and center of the oven and preheat the oven to 325°F. Line 2 rimmed baking sheets with parchment paper.

2. To make the Hot Fudge Sauce, bring the butter, corn syrup, ½ cup water, and sugar to a boil in a heavy medium saucepan over medium-low heat, stirring until the sugar is dissolved. Whisk in the cocoa powder, return to a simmer, and cook, stirring occasionally, until large bubbles form on the surface, about 3 minutes.

3. Put the chocolate in a heatproof bowl. Pour the hot cocoa mixture over the chocolate and let stand until the chocolate softens, about 1 minute. Add the vanilla and salt and whisk until smooth. Place the bowl in a large skillet of gently simmering water over low heat to keep warm.

4. Cut each package of dough into 4 equal pieces to make a total of 8 cookie-dough cylinders. Using a metal spatula, flatten each portion of cookie dough into a disk about 3 inches across and about 1 inch thick. Space the dough evenly and well apart on the prepared baking sheets, as they will spread during baking.

5. Bake for 18 to 20 minutes, switching the positions of the pans from top to bottom and front to back halfway through baking, or until the edges of the cookies are just beginning to brown and the centers still appear to be slightly undercooked. Remove the cookies from the oven and let cool on the pans for 5 to 10 minutes.

6. Using a metal spatula, place a warm cookie into the bottom of a bowl, molding it to fit the shape of the bowl. Repeat to make 8 cookie bowls. Add a generous scoop of ice cream to each cookie bowl, then spoon 3 tablespoons of the hot fudge sauce over the ice cream. Garnish with whipped cream, if you wish. Drizzle additional streaks of hot fudge over the whipped cream. Serve immediately.

# White Chocolate Mousse with Summer Berries

↝ *contributed by* MARCUS MATUSKY

*Not that there is anything wrong with dark chocolate mousse (you can use bittersweet chocolate to replace the white chocolate in this recipe), but this mousse's silky texture and pristine color is irresistible. When purchasing white chocolate, be sure the ingredients include cocoa butter. Tangy fresh berries balance the mousse's sweetness.* {MAKES 8 SERVINGS}

1¼ cups heavy cream

8 ounces high-quality white chocolate, finely chopped

4 large eggs, separated

3 tablespoons confectioners' sugar

4 cups assorted fresh berries, such as raspberries and blueberries

White chocolate curls (see Note, page 204)

↝ **NOTE:** This recipe contains under-cooked eggs, which have been known to carry the potentially harmful salmonella bacterium. Do not serve to the very young or elderly, or anyone with a compromised immune system.

1. Pour ¼ inch water into a medium skillet and bring to a bare simmer over low heat. Pour ¼ cup of the heavy cream into a heatproof small bowl. Add the white chocolate. Place the bowl in the skillet and turn off the heat. Let the chocolate melt, stirring occasionally. Remove the bowl from the heat and let cool slightly.

2. In a medium bowl, whisk the egg yolks until pale yellow and thickened. Gradually whisk in the melted chocolate mixture. Place the bowl in a larger bowl of ice water. Let stand, stirring often, until tepid, about 10 minutes. (If the mixture is too warm, it will melt the whipped cream in the next step.)

3. Beat the remaining 1 cup heavy cream in a chilled medium bowl with an electric mixer on high speed until stiff peaks form. Stir one-quarter of the whipped cream into the white chocolate mixture to lighten its texture. Fold in the remaining cream.

4. Using clean beaters, whip the egg whites in a medium bowl with an electric mixer on high speed until soft peaks form. Add the confectioners' sugar and whip just until the peaks are stiff and shiny. Stir one-quarter of the beaten egg whites into the white chocolate mixture, then fold in the remaining whites.

5. Divide the mousse among 8 individual bowls or wine glasses. Cover each with plastic wrap and refrigerate until chilled and set, at least 3 hours or up to 24 hours. Garnish with berries and white chocolate curls; serve chilled.

# McIntosh Apple Cobbler

*contributed by* MICHAEL LYLE

*An instant classic at our Blue Stove Restaurants, this cobbler is at its best during the apple-harvest season in autumn. McIntosh apples cook to a soft, applesauce-like consistency, but you can also use firmer apples, such as Golden Delicious or Granny Smith, or a combination.* {MAKES 8 SERVINGS}

### APPLE FILLING

6 McIntosh apples, about 2 pounds total, peeled, cored, and cut into ¼-inch-thick wedges

1½ cups sugar

3 tablespoons all-purpose flour

1 tablespoon pure vanilla extract

1 tablespoon ground cinnamon

1 teaspoon ground nutmeg

### COBBLER TOPPING

2 cups all-purpose flour

2 cups sugar

2 teaspoons baking powder

1 teaspoon fine sea salt

½ cup (1 stick) unsalted butter, at room temperature

4 large eggs, beaten

Vanilla ice cream for serving

Ground cinnamon for sprinkling

Store-bought caramel sauce for serving

1. Preheat the oven to 350°F. Butter the bottom and sides of a 13-by-9-inch baking dish.

2. To make the Apple Filling, combine the apples, sugar, flour, vanilla, cinnamon, and nutmeg in a large bowl. Spread evenly in the prepared baking dish.

3. To make the Cobbler Topping, combine the flour, sugar, baking powder, and salt in a medium bowl. Add the butter and eggs. Using a rubber spatula, mix and mash the ingredients together to make a smooth, thick batter. With the spatula, spread the topping in an even layer over the apples and up to the edges of the dish.

4. Put the baking dish on a baking sheet. Bake, rotating the dish after 25 minutes, until the apples are tender and the topping is golden brown, 50 to 55 minutes. Let stand for 30 minutes before serving.

5. For each serving, spoon warm cobbler into a shallow soup bowl. Top with a scoop of ice cream, sprinkle with cinnamon, and drizzle with the caramel sauce. Serve immediately.

# Dark Cherry Crisp

ᴄ✺ *contributed by* MICHAEL NORTHERN

*I am lucky to live in the Pacific Northwest, where cherries are an abundant crop every July and August. Usually, I'm happy eating cherries out of hand, but this crisp provides a fine alternative. It's even better topped with vanilla ice cream.* {MAKES 8 SERVINGS}

### TOPPING

½ cup all-purpose flour

½ cup packed light brown sugar

⅓ cup granulated sugar

1 teaspoon ground cinnamon

¼ teaspoon fine sea salt

Pinch of freshly grated nutmeg

8 tablespoons (1 stick) cold unsalted butter, cut into ½-inch cubes

1 cup old-fashioned rolled oats

### CHERRY FILLING

2 pounds fresh or frozen pitted dark sweet cherries

¾ cup granulated sugar

½ cup apple juice

1 tablespoon fresh lemon juice

½ teaspoon ground ginger

3 tablespoons cornstarch

1. Preheat the oven to 350°F. Line a rimmed baking sheet with aluminum foil. Lightly butter an 11-by-7-inch baking dish.

2. To make the Topping, stir the flour, brown sugar, the ⅓ cup granulated sugar, the cinnamon, salt, and nutmeg together in a bowl. Add the butter and oats. Using your fingers, work in the butter until all the ingredients are well blended but not overmixed. Refrigerate until ready to use.

3. To make the Cherry Filling, bring the cherries, the ¾ cup granulated sugar, the apple juice, lemon juice, and ginger to a simmer in a saucepan over medium heat, stirring occasionally. Simmer for 3 minutes. Meanwhile, pour ¼ cup cold water into a small bowl, sprinkle with the cornstarch, and whisk to dissolve. Stir into the cherry mixture and cook, stirring constantly, until thickened. Pour into the baking dish. Let cool for 15 minutes.

4. Put the baking dish on the prepared baking sheet. Crumble the topping over the cherry mixture. Bake until the topping is brown and crunchy and the cherries are tender, 25 to 30 minutes. Serve the crisp hot, warm, or at room temperature.

# Chocolate Mousse Cake

*contributed by* ROBERT TORNO

*I first learned how to make this seriously chocolate cake from a French chef who taught me to make the most out of a few basic ingredients. I love it because it is easy to make, it serves a large group, and it's always a crowd-pleaser. In fact, it's a bestselling dessert at Nordstrom's Spokane Bistro.*

{MAKES 12 SERVINGS}

### CHOCOLATE CRUST

4 tablespoons plus 1½ teaspoons unsalted butter, melted

20 cream-filled chocolate sandwich cookies

### FILLING

1 pound bittersweet chocolate (no more than 62 percent cacao), coarsely chopped

1¼ cups hot brewed coffee

3¼ cups heavy cream

2½ cups confectioners' sugar

1 tablespoon pure vanilla extract

### TOPPING

¾ cup heavy cream

4 ounces bittersweet chocolate (no more than 62 percent cacao), coarsely chopped

1 tablespoon unsalted butter

1. Preheat the oven to 350°F. Butter the bottom and sides of a 10-by-3-inch springform pan. Line the bottom with a round of parchment paper and brush the paper with a little of the melted butter for the crust.

2. Put the cookies in a 1-gallon lock-top plastic bag and, using a rolling pin, smash them to make coarse crumbs. Working in batches, transfer the coarse crumbs to a food processor and pulse to reduce to fine crumbs. You should have about 2 cups.

3. To make the Chocolate Crust, mix the cookie crumbs and remaining melted butter together in a medium bowl until combined. Press firmly and evenly into the bottom (but not the sides) of the prepared pan. Bake the crust for 10 minutes, or until set. Remove from the oven and set aside.

4. To make the Filling, put the chocolate in a heatproof large bowl. Pour in the hot coffee and let stand for a few minutes to soften the chocolate. Whisk until smooth. Let stand, occasionally whisking the mixture, until it is tepid but still fluid, about 30 minutes.

5. Whip the cream, confectioners' sugar, and vanilla together in a chilled large bowl with an electric mixer set on high speed until the cream just forms stiff peaks. Do not overbeat. Stir about one-fourth of the whipped cream into the tepid chocolate mixture. Add the remaining whipped cream and fold it in. Pour into the springform pan and smooth the top. The pan will be very full, with about ¼ inch clearance from the top. Cover the pan with plastic wrap. Refrigerate until the filling is set, about 2 hours.

*continued >*

6. To make the Topping, heat the cream in a medium saucepan until simmering. Remove from the heat and add the chocolate. Let stand for a few minutes to soften the chocolate. Whisk until smooth, then whisk in the butter. Pour into a small bowl and let stand, whisking occasionally, until tepid, about 15 minutes. Uncover the pan and pour the topping over the filling. Quickly spread with an offset metal spatula into an even layer. Refrigerate, uncovered, until the topping is set, at least 1 hour. (The cake can be refrigerated, loosely covered with plastic wrap without touching the topping, for up to 4 days.)

7. To serve, warm a thin-bladed knife under hot running water and dry the knife. Run the knife around the inside of the pan and remove the sides of the pan. Cut the cake, with the knife heated under hot water and dried before each slicing, and serve chilled.

# Lemon Ricotta Cookies

*contributed by* DANIEL MENCHACA

*Watch out—this cookie, with its enticing flavor and texture, can become addictive. Bite by bite, its sparkling exterior gives way to a fluffy, almost cheesecake-like inside. Note that the cookies are baked from frozen dough, so be sure to clear plenty of room in your freezer and start a day ahead.*

{MAKES 18 COOKIES}

## COOKIES

2½ cups all-purpose flour

1 tablespoon baking powder

1 tablespoon kosher salt

1 cup (2 sticks) unsalted butter, at room temperature

2 cups granulated sugar

2 large eggs

1 pound whole-milk ricotta cheese

Grated zest of 6 lemons

1 tablespoon fresh lemon juice

1. At least 1 day before baking the cookies, make the dough. Sift the flour, baking powder, and salt together into a medium bowl. Beat the butter and granulated sugar together in a large bowl with an electric mixer on high speed until light and fluffy, about 3 minutes. One at a time, beat in the eggs. With the mixer on low speed, in three additions, beat in the ricotta, then the lemon zest and juice. Gradually add the flour mixture and mix just until incorporated. Do not overmix the dough. It will be very soft.

2. Line a baking sheet with parchment paper. Using a 3-ounce-portion ice cream scoop, portion 18 balls of dough onto the baking sheet. Freeze, uncovered, until solid, at least 12 hours. (To store the frozen dough, remove from the baking sheet and transfer to a lock-top freezer bag. Squeeze as much air as possible from the bag, seal, and freeze for up to 2 weeks.)

3. Line 2 rimmed baking sheets with parchment paper. Divide the frozen dough balls among the prepared baking sheets, spacing them about 2 inches apart. Let stand at room temperature until the dough is slightly thawed but still cold and firm, about 30 minutes.

4. Meanwhile, position racks in the top third and center of the oven and preheat the oven to 325°F. Bake the cookies, switching the positions of the pans from top to bottom and front to back halfway through baking, until the edges of the cookies are lightly browned, about 22 minutes. Let the cookies cool on the pans for 5 minutes. Transfer the cookies to wire racks and let cool completely. The icing will melt if the cookies are warm.

*continued >*

### ICING

½ cup (1 stick) unsalted butter,
   at room temperature

3 cups confectioners' sugar, sifted

¼ cup fresh lemon juice

Grated zest of 1 lemon

5. To make the Icing, beat the butter and confectioners' sugar together in a large bowl with an electric mixer on medium speed until well blended. Add the lemon juice and continue mixing until the icing is smooth and about the consistency of cake frosting.

6. Leave the cookies on the wire racks. Use a tablespoon to spoon the icing over the cookies, spreading it in an even, thick layer over three-quarters of the cookie, leaving a ½-inch border at the edge. Grate lemon zest over the center of each cookie. Let the icing set. (The cookies can be stored in an airtight container for up to 2 days, no longer.)

# Index

# Acknowledgments

This cookbook would never have been possible were it not for the outstanding recipe contributions provided by Nordstrom's talented team of food service professionals. Choosing from among the hundreds of submissions was no easy task; there were far too many fantastic dishes to select from. These passionate contributors provided exciting recipes that can perfectly grace your family table: Jeff Barkwill, Tony Colabelli, Ryan Dodge, Sarelle Drought, Peter Dumaliang, Jared Estes, Claire Fankhauser, Rey Garcia, Rob Gibbs, Joan Harnett, Kimberly Hazard, Richard Ladd, Michael Lepage, Jason Longfield, Michael Lyle, Ian MacKinnon, Marcus Matusky, Daniel Menchaca, Sean Miller, Peter O'Keefe, Jonathan Rohland, Vincent Rossetti, Kerri Rupell, Richard Silva, Michael Thoms, Rob Torno, Vicki Wilson, Adam Wohler, Daniel Wood, and Tony Zamora.

I am grateful for all of the support Rick Rodgers provided when it came to the actual writing of this book. Rick has once again drawn upon his hard-earned wisdom to help produce recipes that are easy to follow, filled with practical tips, trustworthy, and, most importantly, always deliver great taste and flavor.

A special thanks is due to Marcus Matusky, who aided me in this project from the very beginning and stayed with me all the way through to its completion. Marcus helped with the initial recipe gathering and editing and then transitioned alongside me to the test kitchen where each and every recipe was tested, sometimes more than once, evaluated, and adjusted for accuracy, clarity, and quality.

I am always thankful for all of the faithful and steadfast support given by Laurel Ewing, who has worked alongside me from our very first book, published in 2003. Laurel's commitment to excellence, her organizational skills, and her attention to detail are qualities that shine through in this work.

The food photography provided by Noel Barnhurst and his sensational team in San Francisco deserves special mention; it just grows from strength to strength. It is so inspiring and reinvigorating to experience the creative teamwork and collaboration that happens in the studio as Noel and his team orchestrate their magic. The creative synergy between George Dolose and Elisabet der Nederlanden in the kitchen, with Noel Barnhurst behind the lens, has resulted in a beautiful collection of images that provides great inspiration to give these dishes a try.

Thank you to the staff at Chronicle Books, including Catherine Huchting, Laurel Leigh, and Pamela Geismar for the expert guidance throughout the evolution of this book. Additionally, thanks to Sara Remington for providing gorgeous garden and farm photos, and to Gretchen Scoble, who went the extra mile to ensure that we ended up with a beautifully designed, terrific-looking book.

Finally, thanks to all of my friends and family who have let me practice dishes for them all of these many years, they are all such a joy to cook for . . .

—Michael Northern